THE TROUBLE

A LIFE OF MARK TWAIN

BEGINS AT 8

THE WILD, WILD WEST

SID FLEISCHMAN

GREENWILLOW BOOKS
An Imprint of HarperCollinsPublishers

The Trouble Begins at 8
A Life of Mark Twain in the Wild, Wild West
Copyright © 2008 by Sid Fleischman

The text of this book is set in Centaur.
Book design by Chad W. Beckerman and Victoria Jamieson.

Library of Congress Cataloging-in-Publication Data
Fleischman, Sid, (date).
The trouble begins at 8 : a life of Mark Twain in the wild, wild
west / by Sid Fleischman.
p. cm.
"Greenwillow Books."
Includes bibliographical references.
ISBN 978-0-06-134431-2 (trade bdg.)
ISBN 978-0-06-134432-9 (lib. bdg.)
1. Twain, Mark, 1835–1910—Childhood and youth—Juvenile
literature. 2. Twain, Mark, 1835–1910—Homes and haunts—
West (U.S.)—Juvenile literature. 3. Authors, American—19th
century—Biography—Juvenile literature.
I. Title. II. Title: Trouble begins at eight.
PS1332F57 2008 818'.409—dc22 [B] 2007037891

13 SCP 10 9 8 7 6
First Edition

Greenwillow Books

For Cheryl Zach, who made a difference,
and for the three Susans:
Hirschman, Erickson, and Chick

CONTENTS

A HORROR OF INTRODUCTIONS

So often had Mark Twain suffered through bumbling introductions before he rose to speak that he sometimes chose to introduce himself. "I was obliged to excuse the chairman from introducing me, because he never compliments anybody and I knew I could do it just as well," he began a speech in San Francisco, and he lavished witty praise on the evening's speaker—himself.

He was bested only once, when a miner in Nevada was charged with performing the welcome. "I don't know anything about this man. I only know two things about him. One is, he has never been in jail. And the other is, I don't know why."

For the past hundred years, the famous author has been known everywhere but on the dark side of the moon. An introduction would be redundant. I'll confine myself, therefore, to an offstage note or two.

When I was the young writer of a novel, *The New York Times* reviewed my comedy with the news that I was no Mark Twain. I was astonished. I had already had myself fitted for a white suit, like the celebrated author of *Tom Sawyer* and *Huckleberry Finn*. I had been trying to track down the brand of cigars he smoked by the handful. His wit may have come from the noxious weed. Who knew?

Genius is not catching, like the measles. No one will ever be another Mark Twain. But he is in the DNA of every modern American writer. He loosened up the language for us. He gave us our unique sense of humor.

As one who has spent a lifetime at a writer's desk, I felt that I could give insights to a Twain biography that may have eluded the scholarly academics who had cleared the way for me. I could sense why he had so much trouble plotting a novel. It happens to us lesser fry. We could understand his conjuring trick of changing real life into real fiction.

I have chosen to write about the adventurous years that turned the unknown Samuel Clemens into the world-famous Mark Twain.

It was during these early years, culminating in a San Francisco hotel, that he gathered the driftwood that would fuel his most celebrated novels. His life that followed in the East, as a squire with a houseful of servants, had the character of curtain calls.

The white-haired man in the white suit would have immediately recognized the title of this biography. When Twain began speaking in public, his first poster proclaimed that the doors would open at seven. "The Trouble to begin at 8 o'clock."

Turn the page and the trouble will get under way.

CHAPTER ONE
THE MAN WHO MADE FROGS FAMOUS

ARK TWAIN WAS BORN FULLY GROWN, WITH A cheap cigar clamped between his teeth.

The event took place, as far as is known, in a San Francisco hotel room sometime in the fall of 1865. The only person attending was a young newspaperman and frontier jester named Samuel Langhorne Clemens.

Who?

A person of little consequence. He was a former tramp printer, Mississippi riverboat pilot, and ink-stained scribbler who'd made a small noise in the brand-new Nevada Territory.

Sam, or even Sammy, as boyhood friends and relatives sometimes called him, sat in the light from the hotel window scratching out a comic story about a jumping frog contest. He'd discovered the bleached ribs of the story not far off, in the California Gold Rush foothills. He now set the tale in his native folk language. He gave the story fresh and whimsical orchestration. He made it art.

He rummaged around among several pen names with which he'd amused himself in the past. Newspaper humorists, such as his friends Petroleum V. Nashby and Dan De Quille, commonly hid in the shade of absurd false fronts. Should he be Josh again? Thomas J. Snodgrass? Mark Twain? How about W. Epaminondas Blab?

Mark Twain. It recalled a shouted refrain from his riverboat days, signifying a safe water depth of two fathoms, or twelve feet. He'd given the pen name a trial run on a political scribble or two, but the name had only enhanced his obscurity. He had let it molder and die.

Still, he would feel cozy under the skin of a character from his beloved Mississippi River. Maybe he'd blow on its ashes and resurrect the pseudonym. With earnest decision, a possible snort, and a flourish of his pen, he signed the piece, "By Mark Twain."

Nothing traveled fast in those days except the common cold. But once the celebrated frog of Calaveras County reached the East

Coast and was reprinted by newspapers large and small, the nation had seizures of giggles and guffaws. The merriment spread with the swiftness of a gale-force wind. The story crossed the Atlantic Ocean, and before long the English and later the French "most killed themselves laughing" as Twain reported, falling back on his Missouri drawl.

Today, we are still smiling out loud at how Smiley lost the frog-jumping contest to a stranger with a secret cache of buckshot.

Mark Twain had made the overstuffed amphibian famous. At first, the creature had grabbed the spotlight exclusively for himself. The author reacted with a bilious grunt of jealousy toward his creation. Complained Twain, "It was only the frog that was celebrated. It wasn't I."

But soon Mark Twain caught up, sprinting past the croaker to become the most famous American alive. And the funniest.

Each chomping simultaneously on the same cigar, Sam Clemens and Mark Twain conspired to write what many regard as America's greatest novels, *Adventures of Huckleberry Finn* and its companion *The Adventures of Tom Sawyer*. And that's not to mention the knock-about pages of *Life on the Mississippi* or the fanciful *The Prince and the*

Pauper, a novel about two look-alikes who exchange places, with results you can imagine. An unending carnival of movies, plays, and Broadway musicals have been spun off from Mark Twain's rowdy comedies and satires.

From under the author's full mustache, hanging like a rusted scimitar over his sharp quips, came an evergreen stream of wit. His sayings remain as perky today as when Twain first minted them. "Man is the only animal who blushes, or needs to," said he. "Cauliflower is nothing but cabbage with a college education." "Everybody complains about the weather, but nobody does anything about it."

Not bad for a barefoot boy with a prairie fire of curly red hair who was born in Florida, a Missouri village so small that Sam remembered it as "almost invisible." Halley's comet was streaking across the sky like a chalk mark the day he was born. Seventy-five years later, it came blazing back, as if by personal invitation—the day the celebrated author snubbed out his cigar and moved in with the immortals.

But there was something more remarkable afoot in Florida, Missouri, the day Sam added himself to the world's population.

Destiny had searched out the obscure village of twenty-one homes for a flash of its rarest lightning—genius.

Sam was struck in the funny bone. Burdened with literary imagination and originality, he grew up to snatch the dust covers and embroidered antimacassars off the novels of the day. He changed literature forever. He scraped earth under its fingernails and taught it to spit. He slipped in a subversive American sense of humor. He made laughing out loud as respectable as afternoon tea.

CHAPTER TWO
EGGS, THREE CENTS A DOZEN

IF ANYONE HAD POSTED A SIGN AT THE MUDDY city limits of Florida, Missouri (assuming the place had adopted airs and boasted of city limits), outstretched index fingers would have pointed to the west and the east.

    ☜ INDIAN TERRITORY 200 MILES

    ☞ MISSOURI RIVER 30 MILES

After going to a lot of trouble to be born there, two months premature, frail and sickly, on a bleak November 30 in 1835, Sam Clemens grew up to discover his future in both directions.

That he grew up at all was his first adventure in confounding

MARK TWAIN BIRTHPLACE, FLORIDA, MO.

As a child, Mark Twain thought he was born in a palace. Years later, revisiting the place, he was astonished to see that his birthplace in Florida, Missouri, was a mere cabin. As for the visitor shown here, his identity is unknown.

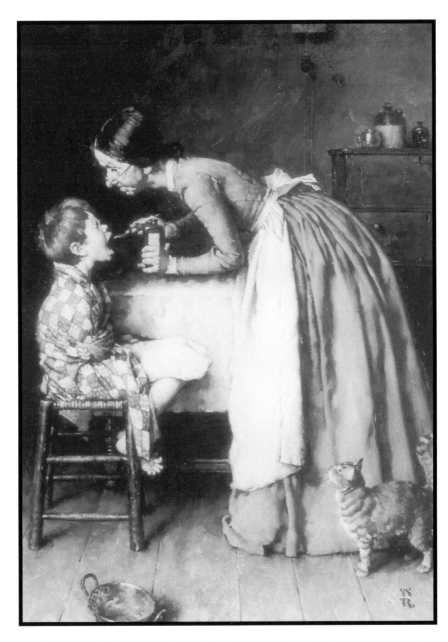

Mark Twain confessed to generously sharing his doses of medicine, when no one was looking, with the family cats.

the odds. Said his mother, "When I first saw him, I saw no promise in him."

During the ailing first seven years of his life, Sam consumed enough medicine, particularly castor oil, to kill a mule. Later, he confessed to pouring as much as he could down the throats of the nineteen household cats, strays that his older brother Orion kept dragging home.

Family doctors then charged twenty-five dollars a year to treat an entire family and threw in the medicines free. Doses of calomel, the popular cure-all, were apt to attack the teeth. Worry not: the doctor also pulled teeth. Said Twain, "If the jaw remained, it wasn't his fault."

Having been close to death several times, Twain asked his mother in her old age, "I suppose that during all that time you were uneasy about me?"

"Yes, the whole time."

"Afraid I wouldn't live?"

Something of a wit herself, Mrs. Clemens replied, "No—afraid you would."

His father John, a self-educated attorney with few clients, was a get-rich-quick dreamer. He spent a lifetime chasing bluebirds that turned out to be trashy mockingbirds.

Twain could not recall ever hearing his father laugh. John Clemens tried to invent a perpetual-motion machine that, once started, would run on nothing but pure Missouri air. Its failure allowed him time to invest in silkworms, whose stylish fiber might rival cotton in southern agriculture. The silkworms ate up his bankroll instead.

He abandoned Florida in Sam's fourth year. The boy would miss his friends, especially warm and wise Uncle Dan'l, a slave on Sam's uncle's farm. Writing as Mark Twain years later, he rendered Uncle Dan'l into one of the most celebrated and treasured characters in literature—Jim, the runaway slave in *Huckleberry Finn*.

After the sudden death of a daughter, John Clemens moved his family, plus the slave girl, Jennie, to Hannibal, a hilly port city on the Mississippi River. The get-rich-quick fortune he sought would be there, but it would skip a generation. It was Sam who harvested the plunder lying about in the dusty streets of Hannibal. Only an imaginative boy could detect the glint of treasure.

John Clemens, who opened a general store and sold eggs for

Twain used a vast and winding limestone cave two miles south of his hometown as the setting for spooky scenes in *Tom Sawyer*. In this original illustration from the first edition of the novel, Tom and Becky Thatcher get separated from friends and lost.

The same scene as staged for a motion-picture version. The art director loyally
followed the book.

three cents a dozen and whiskey for ten cents a gallon, could hardly have chosen a better stage set for his gifted son to perform his boyhood dramas.

Sam got lost in a vast and mysterious cave sheltering a murderer and hiding buried treasure. He could climb a tall bluff to gaze across the mile-wide river to the dark shore of Illinois. One of the author's young heroes was the son of the town drunk. There was a whitewashed fence that Twain would make as famous as the Great Wall of China.

Above all, there was the river itself, with its whistling steamboats, its river tramps and scamps and its rafts dreamily floating on the current like log carpets. A boy could hoist a lantern and live aboard such a craft and see the fabled world beyond the next bend or two.

Twain put it all in his books, and himself as well. He confessed to having been partly the live model for Tom Sawyer, the hero of his first great novel. Tom became the dream image of American country boyhood: barefooted, carefree, smiling under a ragged straw farm hat, primed for the day's adventure with a fishing pole across one shoulder.

But hovering over this scene of innocence came the lightning flashes and the rolling thunder of slavery. Growing up with a mind of his own, Twain would make a clean break from the birthright bigotry of his neighbors. Wrote he, "In my schoolboy days I had no aversion to slavery. I was not aware there was anything wrong about it. No one arraigned it in my hearing; the local papers said nothing against it; the local pulpit taught us that God approved it, that it was a holy thing and that the doubter need only look in the Bible if he wished to settle his mind."

Sam's see-through mind was beginning to perceive a conspiracy of delusion and evil. He would come to arrive at a low opinion of the human race and to write, "Man—a creature made at the end of the week's work when God was tired." He regretted that our biblical ancestors hadn't missed the boat when Noah was boarding passengers.

He was a skinny eight-year-old on a chilly October night when he witnessed a procession of religious cultists in white robes holding aloft pitch-pine torches as they climbed Lover's Leap to await the end of the world. The possibility that if they were right, he wouldn't have to go to school the next day must have eased his mind.

The spooky vision on the high bluff just north of town festered among his memories, and no doubt enriched his scorn for religion's mischiefs. Never one to let human folly escape his pen, Twain found a place for the scene in a long-planned sequel to *Huckleberry Finn*. The novel was left unwritten only by his death.

While illiteracy was going out of fashion, it still thrived around him, as common as dirt. No public schools yet existed in Missouri. Ignorance was cheap. There was a price tag on learning. Private schools charged a great sum—twenty-five cents per student per week. Kids continued to be bred to work on the farms, not to learn history and to recite highfalutin' poetry. You didn't need geometry in order to plow a straight furrow in a cornfield.

Sam regarded it as akin to child abuse that his father, elected justice of the peace, scraped up the funds to send him to the log schoolhouse at the edge of town, there to be tamed. He was four and a half years old, troublesome, busy, and with an imagination in constant flight. His war with formal education had begun.

CHAPTER THREE
THE GINGERBREAD KID

I T WAS COMMONLY HELD ON THE FRESHLY PLOWED frontier that anyone who could count to twenty without taking off his shoes was qualified to teach school. William H. McGuffey, whose famous reading series—McGuffey Readers—tutored Sam in the art of unpuzzling the printed word, himself had been permitted to teach school in Ohio at the age of thirteen.

Sam's first teacher was more formidable, a no-nonsense, middle-aged Yankee lady in a bonnet with lace trim. She wore small glasses through which she could detect mischief still in its larval stage. Sam was twice punished on his first day at school for committing felonies he was unaware of. The thought that a boy needed a lawyer to acquire an education may have begun his souring on formal schooling and his preference for teaching himself.

But there, in the schoolhouse, Mrs. Horr balanced his dismay with the stunning news that prayer did, indeed, work. Sam decided to give it a test. He prayed for gingerbread.

Behold!

The treat appeared. The daughter of the town baker had brought a slice of gingerbread to sustain her, and "she was looking the other way." Sam availed himself of God's prompt gift to a hungry boy.

"I was a convert," Twain said. "I did as much praying during the next two or three days as anyone in that town." But he was never again able to bring forth a slab of gingerbread by prayer. His faith was wounded.

It was at school that Sam sustained his most humiliating putdown. An older girl in a sunbonnet and calico dress confronted him. She asked him if he chewed tobacco.

No, he confessed.

"It roused her scorn. She reported me to all the crowd and said, 'Here's a boy seven years old who can't chaw tobacco.'

"By the looks and comments which this produced I realized that

I was a degraded object. I was cruelly ashamed of myself. I determined to reform."

He bit off mouthfuls of tobacco and chomped away, sure to win respect. Instead, he got sick to his stomach. He was almost as backward when he took up smoking. He was a late-blooming nine.

"But a boy's life is not all comedy," he would write, looking back on the day he ditched school until dark. On his way home, where his mother would be waiting, he passed his father's office. "Because I had a delicacy about . . . getting thrashed," he climbed through a window and stretched out on the couch.

Unknown to him, there had been a stabbing in the street, and lacking a morgue, the town had commandeered the Clemens office to harbor the bloody deceased.

Sam's eyes began picking out details in the dark. "I fancied I could see a long, dusky, shapeless thing stretched upon the floor. A cold shiver ran through me. I turned my face to the wall. That did not answer. I was afraid that that thing would creep over and seize me in the dark."

Presently the moon rose like a stage prop to throw a windowpane of light across the body. A dead hand, white as a cotton glove, now

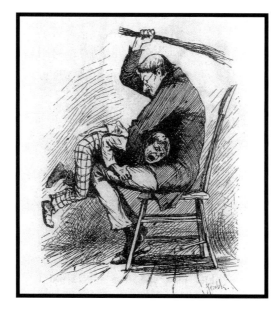

Twain was punished on his first day of school, an experience he slipped into the pages of *Huckleberry Finn*.

The Clemens home in Hannibal, freshly painted for tourists.

Huckleberry Finn ambled onto the world stage with a dead cat in his hand. Twain often gave his characters dramatic entrances.

appeared. Sam gasped for breath and sat up. Now the moonlight revealed a naked arm, the knife wound in the chest, and the eyes, "fixed and glassy in death."

Sam's heart leaped into his throat. "I went out at the window, and I carried the sash along with me. I did not need the sash, but it was handier to take it than it was to leave it, and so I took it."

His punishment at home steadied his nerves. His school attendance improved.

Learning to read was the momentous event in Sam's life. It would soon enable him to breach the borders of Hannibal and to shake hands with the world at large. He mastered the printed page in lightning storms of boyish curiosity. With a memory well stocked with flypaper, he could reel off whole pages from tales of adventure. He could spell almost as well as the dictionary and triumphantly walked away with all the school spelling prizes. Words were a conjuration, and their charms had begun to bewitch him.

But being caged in the schoolhouse when the birds were twittering outside and the splash of the riverboat paddlewheels sounded in his ears, as festive as calliopes—this daily confinement was curdling his boyhood.

He became restless. He became even more troublesome. He ditched school to go roaming, sometimes with his notorious but envied friend Tom Blankenship. The unwashed outcast of Hannibal, son of the town drunk, Tom had never been to school. He was a free spirit, permitted by neglect to bring himself up. Doomed by illiteracy, he survived the paradise of a charmed boyhood to vanish in adulthood. It is not even known where his bones are buried. But he hovers like a ghost over the pages of an irrepressible storybook adventure after Mark Twain changed Tom's name to Huckleberry Finn and made him the most amusing, subversive, and envied child in literature.

After ten years or so of education by rote and boredom, Sam escaped the schoolhouse forever. But his learning had just begun.

His father died. Sam burst into tears of remorse for his years of untamed disobedience. His mother opened her arms to comfort him.

"It is all right, Sammy," she said. "Now I want you to promise me—"

"I'll promise anything," he sobbed, "if you won't make me go to school! Anything!"

It must have amazed him to hear her say, "No, Sammy; you need not go to school anymore. Only promise me to be a better boy. Promise not to break my heart."

At least, that's the story of the abrupt end of his formal education that Twain told his scribbling biographer, Albert Bigelow Paine. Twain appears to have improved on the facts in the drama, for Sam was still in school two years later. An explanation for this discrepancy may be found in his mother's remark about her gifted son, "I discount him ninety percent for embroidery, and what is left is perfect and priceless truth."

That night, after the funeral, Sam walked in his disordered sleep. With a white sheet thrown over him, he awakened and terrified his mother and sister until his face appeared.

He walked again and again on the following nights. No one has calculated how many miles in his young life this nightwalker adventured on the family floorboards. Was he trying to escape?

When he quit school at last, he walked out of his boyhood. Tripping over his own bare feet, he stumbled into adulthood.

CHAPTER FOUR
UPSIDE DOWN AND BACKWARD

SAM LANDED A DREAM JOB. HE WAS FOURTEEN years old, as Mark Twain was later to calculate. Scholars question his arithmetic. They add a couple of years.

Apprenticed to a printer who published one of the two Hannibal newspapers, the *Courier,* he had the privilege of sweeping up, of running and fetching, and even of learning to set newspaper type—all without being burdened with a salary. Not a cent.

But he was allowed to sleep on the floor, free of charge. And he would be provided with a suit of clothes—a ragged garment previously lived in and worn out by the editor and publisher, Joseph Ament. Wrote Twain: "I was only half as big as Ament, consequently his shirts gave me the uncomfortable sense of living in a

The only picture that has survived of Mark Twain as a kid and a printer's devil, a term for apprentices. Here he's often regarded as fourteen. Pridefully holding a typestick, he has arranged woodblock letters to spell Sam.

Mark Twain's mother

This is presumed to be Twain's boyhood bedroom.

circus tent, and I had to turn up his pants to my ears to make them short enough."

California madness gripped Hannibal, for the Gold Rush had burst upon the nation. Tales of the discovery of yellow nuggets at the edge of the American River kept Sam busy at the typecases. He was not among the fevered local citizens to rough it across the two thousand miles of prickly Wild West in 1849 to strike it rich. The California madness would have to wait until Sam was fully grown.

Meanwhile, the tightfisted wife of the publisher provided meals notable for their trifling portions. News of the great potato famine then raging in Ireland could not have escaped backwater Hannibal, and Sam must have felt himself to be a cosufferer. To sustain himself, Sam felt obliged to raid the cellar at night for potatoes and other farm sass taken in barter for subscriptions.

In exchange for the publisher's pinchpenny largesse, he was initiated into the printer's craft. Standing on a wooden box for height, he quickly mastered the art of hand-setting type. Words now acquired weight. Each magic letter was cast in silvery lead, bright as winter sunshine. With a typestick in one hand, Sam learned to read his native language upside down and backward.

A protective arm clutched the now-bereaved Clemens family. Older by ten years, Sam's fickle brother Orion took charge. Named after the brilliant constellation of the great hunter of Greek mythology, he bore little resemblance to the dashing hero in the sky. The family even insisted on accenting the first syllable, mispronouncing his name as "Oh'rion" (instead of O-rí-on"). He was already a printer in St. Louis and began sending home money.

Orion had a passion for alchemy, but he got the formula wrong. He kept turning gold into lead. He borrowed five hundred dollars and bought a weekly newspaper, the *Hannibal Journal*. It was a blunder.

But not for Sam, who was delighted now to be in the employ of his brother, who had lured him away from the *Courier* with a blissful promise of $3.50 a week. Alas, as Orion's paper struggled to stay alive through the years, the paychecks, week by week, failed to show up—ever.

But Sam had a chance to assume the tempting role of published author, poet, and newspaperman. Depending heavily on national news, Orion rarely chose to run local doings in his paper, nor had humor crossed his sober mind.

The adventuring boys in Twain's novels preferred climbing in and out of windows rather than using front doors.

Needing to be in St. Louis, Orion left his young brother in charge of the paper. Sam was quick to draw upon instinct and give the subscribers something to laugh at. He wrote:

TERRIBLE ACCIDENT!
500 men killed and missing!!!

In modest type he added:

We had set the above head up, expecting (of course)

to use it, but as the accident hasn't happened, yet,

we'll say (To be continued.)

As for local news, why not start a feud with the editor of the competing paper, the *Tri-Weekly Messenger*? Wasn't this in the tradition of frontier journalism, when an editor was presumed to carry a weapon at all times and to be able to pick his teeth with it? Sam charged the editor with "failing to drink himself to death" and other misdemeanors.

When the enraged editor discovered that his adversary was

hardly more than a school brat, the redheaded Clemens boy, he exploded but retreated in humiliation.

Returning to Hannibal, Orion discovered his young brother's mischief. Smoke shot out of his ears. But a sudden increase in subscribers put out the fire. Still, the newspaper could barely keep ahead of its persistent bills.

Sam put up with his hard-earned penury until he no longer needed to stand on a box to set type. He was seventeen or so when he packed a suitcase and set out to see the big cities. But not before his mother nailed his hand to the family Bible.

"I want you to repeat after me, Sam, these words," she said. "I do solemnly swear that I will not throw a card or drink a drop of liquor while I am gone."

That might not be the most festive of adieux, but Sam already knew plenty about swearing, and here was one suitable for framing. He solemnly swore, and kept his word to neither play cards nor drink while on his travels.

As a skilled printer, he was able to find work wherever he rambled—from St. Louis to New York City.

As had Orion, Sam inherited from his father a delusional eye for undiscovered wealth lying about. In due time, swinging back west to the Mississippi River, he came down with a fresh get-rich-quick scheme.

Not silkworms. Not perpetual machines. Sam got Amazon fever. "I made up my mind to go to the headwaters of the Amazon and collect coca and trade in it and make a fortune."

Paying sixteen dollars for a passage to New Orleans, he boarded a ramshackle old riverboat, the *Paul Jones*. Once ashore, he went looking for a ship to Brazil. He was confounded to discover "that there weren't any and learned that there probably wouldn't be any during that century."

While Clemens was marooned in New Orleans with little cash, a new and grandiose idea sprang into his head. He headed back to the *Paul Jones* and climbed to the glass box of the pilothouse. There stood Horace Bixby, one of the pilots, an explosive little man. Sam, consigned to the printer's trade, was about to trump destiny.

CHAPTER FIVE
THE RIVERBOAT RAJAH

EVERY SHIRTTAIL BOY GROWING UP ON THE BANKS of the Mississippi regarded riverboat pilots as first cousins to the gods. Strutting around with the arrogance of peacocks, these men had pounded into their memories every bend and landmark, every sunken wreck, sandbar, and barking dog in the longest river in the country. Sam Clemens, in company with other worshipful boys, had dreamed of becoming a dashing prince of the river, a steamboat pilot.

Aboard the *Paul Jones*, Sam boldly introduced himself to the pilot, the peppery Horace Bixby. "How would you like a young man to learn the river?" he asked.

"I wouldn't like it," Bixby replied sharply. "Cub pilots are more trouble than they're worth."

Always courteous, Sam persisted, and Bixby spared him a withering look.

"Do you drink?" asked the riverboat rajah.

"No."

"Do you swear?"

"Not for amusement; only under pressure."

Bixby almost smiled. He became civil. "There is only one way I would take a young man to learn the river: that is, for money."

"What do you charge?"

Five hundred dollars, came the answer.

Sam didn't fall over dead. That was enough greenbacks to choke a horse, but he was undaunted. Perhaps his generous brother-in-law, upriver in St. Louis, might be persuaded to put up a down payment.

Sam proposed a counteroffer. "I'll give you one hundred dollars cash and the rest when I earn it."

Although having the social graces of a wood file, Bixby was an experienced judge of character. Here was a boy with a country voice as down-home as cornbread. He was eager, earnest, polite, and clearly intelligent. And the pilot had a sore foot. It would be a relief to have a cub pilot stand at the wheel for him. He agreed to teach Sam the cunning perils of twelve hundred miles of the river, as tangled as a tapeworm, for the hundred dollars cash down, payable when they reached St. Louis.

Sam spent the next two years attached to Bixby like a leech. He launched himself on a prodigious feat of memory, trying to fix the great Mississippi River in his head: every bend, every snag, every hill, every sycamore and China tree to sight by; every bayou, every island, both bare and towheaded with cottonwoods, every invisible fathom and every sunken ship's wreck—there were a thousand of them. He must learn his way on the blackest night and in white fogs.

So that steamboats might avoid charging into one another, the river was regarded as a two-way artery. Once Sam had mastered the channels upriver from New Orleans to St. Louis, he needed to undertake the other side of the confounded river, all the way back down.

During his first days aboard, when Bixby pointed out the passing vistas, Sam assumed he was merely making polite conversation. Later his tutor asked, "What's the name of the first point above New Orleans?"

The hot-tempered Horace Bixby, here posing with warm-hearted calm, taught Twain every bend and shallow of the fickle Mississippi River.

The safety of the boat depended on the leadsman. He'd throw a lead weight over the side to discover how far below lay the river bottom, to avoid running aground. He'd call out readings to the pilot. The yell of "Mark twain!" had a joyous sound. It meant a safe depth of twelve feet.

Steamboat captains had a passion for racing one another and blowing their ships to pieces. A great underwater armada of ghost ships with exploded boilers lies on the river bottom. Twain had to learn to steer around these hazards, even in fogs and at night.

Sam replied that he didn't know.

"Don't *know*? Well, you're a smart one. What's the name of the *next* point?"

Sam hadn't a clue. Perhaps he should have been paying attention as Bixby pointed out the river sights.

The pilot exploded. "You're the stupidest dunderhead I ever saw or heard of, so help me Moses! The idea of *you* being a pilot—*you!* Why, you don't know enough to pilot a cow down a lane."

Sam got hold of a notebook and eventually filled several of them with precise river geography. To his own surprise, he developed a great affection for his imperial instructor, whose bristling manner concealed a sly sense of humor.

At a point in his education when Sam was confident that he had the river tamed in his mind and that he could pilot every hazard with his eyes shut, Bixby decided to test him with a practical joke.

The great pilot conspired with the leadsman stationed at the bow. He asked the crewman to call out false readings as he plumbed the water depth with a line weighted at the tip with lead.

Sam, at the wheel, had no doubt that he had the ship in a channel so deep that he "couldn't get the bottom there with a church steeple."

But the leadsman was calling out shallow and shallower depths.

"Mark twain! Half twain! Quarter twain!"

The bottom was rising to grab the ship's bottom. Sam panicked, screaming into the brass speaking tube to the engineer below. "Oh, Ben, if you love me, *back* her! Quick, Ben! Oh, back the immortal *soul* out of her!"

A roar of shipboard laughter roiled the air, and Bixby materialized to give the hoax its point. At the wheel, his cub knew he was in deep water. Bixby shouted that he should have allowed nothing to rattle his confidence. A pilot must forever be loyal to the iron-clad accuracy of his river memory.

Sam learned his lesson. But for weeks he had to endure the humiliation of a phrase that became a daily shipboard taunt. "Oh, Ben, if you love me, *back* her!"

CHAPTER SIX

THE CRUEL RIVER

THE STEAMBOAT WAS CHANGING EVERYTHING. IN an age when log rafts and keelboats were regarded as the cutting edge of river travel, the great wonder machines burst upon the Mississippi frontier. Smoking like house fires, they were high tech decked out as gingerbread palaces. They made old times obsolete.

These belching monsters of wheels and gears and paddles and boilers and live steam were the new pack animals. With ships' bells clanging and whistles piercing the air, they whisked Southern cotton to New England and London top hats to Missouri.

Sam arrived on the noisy scene in the nick of time. The great age of steamboating soon would be virtually dry-docked. In 1859, on the occasion of being certified as a genuine river pilot, the ambitious boy from Hannibal was justifiably happy with himself. He had ascended to the river nobility.

For the first time in his hardscrabble life, at age twenty-three, he felt rich. The customary pilot's pay was $250 a month, equal to the salary of the vice president of the United States. He was able to send money home and to pay off his debt to Horace Bixby.

His pockets weighted with gold, he bought himself a silk top hat and briefly grew out muttonchop whiskers in the latest style. This gave him the general appearance of having a whimsical case of the mumps, and they soon disappeared.

Could life be any better? A pilot and his hawk's eye were needed afloat, but once the boat snuggled up to the wharves in St. Louis or New Orleans, Clemens would leap ashore. While the crew was hard at work discharging or loading cargo, the loose-limbed, tangle-haired pilot became a gentleman of leisure in the great cities. He was not likely to be seen again, Twain confessed, "till the last bell was ringing and everything in readiness for another voyage."

But river life was fickle and notoriously cruel. The floating palaces were built for quick and easy profits, not for safety.

Sam was not to escape the river's sudden treacheries.

A submerged tree could rip open a ship's fragile bottom. The boats collided like snorting bulls and sank. They were firetraps. Their huge boilers, as touchy as volcanoes, exploded. One steersman claimed to have been blown through his pilothouse roof three times. "It was a large experience," he added.

Enter tragedy. Twain persuaded his brother Henry, younger by three years, to abandon the print shop for the Mississippi. The youth began his training aboard a riverboat as a mud clerk—a rank beginner. He'd receive no pay aboard the *Pennsylvania*, but the service would qualify him for the next step up the river ladder.

Near Memphis, the *Pennsylvania* blew up.

Henry was flung high, caught in live steam and fire. His lungs were scorched.

Sam rushed to the scene. When he saw his kid brother, he collapsed in a heap.

Henry died after six days, possibly of a disputed overdose of morphine to ease the pain, administered at Sam's insistence.

Dazed with grief, Sam blamed himself. If he hadn't lured Henry to river life, his younger brother would be alive and smiling.

St. Louis, as Mark Twain saw it while approaching to find space for his ship along the crowded wharves. Like suckling pigs, steamboats were clustered in a row a mile long before the great city.

Twain was a young dandy on the river. When he tried wearing trendy muttonchop whiskers, he appeared to have a whimsical case of the mumps.

Guilt hounded him for the rest of his life. Years after the tragedy, when he sat down to write his heavily autobiographical novel *The Adventures of Tom Sawyer*, he gave his bad hero a good younger half-brother, Sid. Later, he would add, "But Sid was not Henry. Henry was a very much finer and better boy than ever Sid was."

Mark Twain's younger brother, Henry (shown above), died in a ship's explosion much like this one. He was nineteen years old.

CHAPTER SEVEN
SAM AND THE FORTUNE-TELLER

IN NEW ORLEANS, CLEMENS PASSED A SCHOOL promising to teach foreign languages, one for $25, three for $50. Who could ignore a nifty bargain like that?

River life gave the young pilot time to polish his skills as an autodidact, one eager to teach himself. He walked in and signed up at once for French, German, and Italian. He was given phrase cards to study in each language. After a few weeks, he decided he could do without German gutturals and the operatic vowels of Italian. But he remained loyal to the French, and years later, on a visit to France, he was disappointed when he spoke French that he never succeeded "in making those idiots understand their own language."

Clemens seems to have been born ravenous for knowledge. Now he took leaps into the works of the greatest authors and thinkers. He read *Don Quixote*, the tale of a mad Spanish gentleman who believes himself to be a knight on a chivalrous quest for glory. Sam swallowed Shakespeare's plays, one by one, like beefsteaks. He found time for Greek history, for the sciences, but with the Bible always within reach. Late in his steamboating career, he bumped into the theory of evolution and read Darwin for himself in the freshly published bombshell *On the Origin of Species*. He had already been having doubts about a Hebrew-speaking snake slithering through the garden of Eden and that showstopper about Adam's rib being turned into Eve.

Sam had inherited the common homegrown bigotries and deep-fried religious absolutes. Like all those about her, his otherwise kind and compassionate mother believed that the Bible gave its divine stamp of approval to slavery. Sam had grown up as familiar with the whitewashed landscapes of Heaven and the fire pits of Hell as with the weedy lanes of Hannibal. He had never troubled to examine the common beliefs, gift wrapped, that had been consigned to him.

But onboard ship, he found himself reading the rebellious work of the patriot and conscience of the American Revolution, Thomas Paine. It disturbed Clemens to discover that his village mind had never entertained an original or questioning thought. He had allowed the convictions of others to settle in like squatters. Now he'd found a bloodshot eye-opener and a noisy hero.

Slavery? How could a benevolent God so punish a race for its color that He Himself had created?

Sam recalled thundering nights, when he burrowed in terror under the covers: The banging and cracking in the sky he knew to be Jehovah looking to give small Sam Clemens a celestial horse-whipping for his horrendous naughtiness. Why would a punishing God, the one he found extolled in church every Sunday, have searched him out, a sickly little pipsqueak in Hannibal, Missouri, for His personal wrath?

Now he began to question everything but gravity. In time, he came to a conviction about the eternal prairie fires below, waiting for sinners. He confessed, "I don't believe in Hell, but I'm afraid of it."

He would later admit that it was an act of isolated and lonely courage to publicly abuse the received faith and follies of pre–Civil

War America. He was saved from tar and featherings, and even a public noose or two, by the brilliance of his wit and humor. How do you hang a man who keeps you laughing?

Meanwhile, river life continued to bedazzle him. "I loved the profession far better than any I have followed since," he would write. He remained confident of his own future: He intended to follow the Mississippi for the rest of his working life.

Perhaps in search of a second opinion, he consulted a celebrated New Orleans fortune-teller. The young and tiny Madame Caprell, he wrote, had dark hair and black eyes to peer into the future. She buried her pretty face in her hands and then let loose a hurricane of divinations. She revealed that he was off the water. (Who but a riverboat noble would be wearing patent-leather shoes and a hat smartly tilted?) He would follow the great river for another ten years, she prophesied. (Bad guess.)

He was powerfully addicted to tobacco, said she. (True. The aroma of cigars clung to his clothes like a mist.) The only thing that may have confused her was the cheapness of his smokes. He'd developed a taste for trash cigars as a boy and preferred them to expensive brands to the end of his life.

"You are self-made."

"You flatter well, Madame," Sam replied.

"Don't interrupt."

She got a few things right. There had been a death in the family (a one-size-fits-all psychic revelation). He should have trained as a lawyer. There his talents would distinguish him as an orator, she promised.

Sam was always curious about the weird sciences, such as hypnotism and phrenology, a fakery that assessed the character by bumps on the head. Years later in London, Twain's skepticism would be confirmed when a famous phrenologist examined Twain's skull only to discover a total lack of the bump signifying humor.

Paying Madame Caprell her two-dollar fee, he described the event as "just as good as going to the opera." He saw through the fortune-telling game as simpleminded trickery and later wrote, "Prophecy: Two bull's-eyes out of a possible million." He credited her only with being smart.

He had become aware that like all experienced clairvoyants, Madame Caprell could extract information as deftly as a pickpocket. She could read signs: his small-town speech, his nouveau

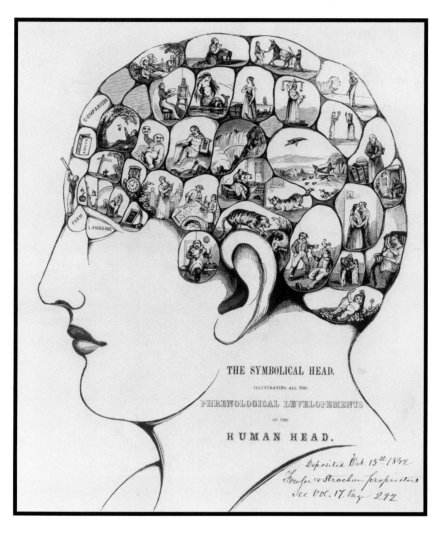

THE SYMBOLICAL HEAD.

ILLUSTRATING ALL THE

PHRENOLOGICAL DEVELOPEMENTS

OF THE

HUMAN HEAD.

Deposited Oct. 15th 1842
Fowler & Strachan proprietors
See Vol. 17. Pag. 292

Twain took a skeptical interest in fortune-telling. Later, he visited a phrenologist, who presumed to read one's character and future by examining the bumps on one's head. The oracle told the author that he was missing a bump signifying a sense of humor. Twain signified phrenology a public fraud.

riche clothes, his resonant voice suggesting a career in the law or on the platform. She knew how to transform these stolen crumbs into occult revelations.

But she had failed to foretell the explosive event that really lay directly ahead for Sam and for herself. She hadn't a clue that within two months, the Civil War would be in everyone's future.

CHAPTER EIGHT
TWO WEEKS AS A WARRIOR

MARK TWAIN'S BATTLE CAREER WAS DISTINGUISHED only by the dash and spunk with which he made his retreat.

He was a steamship passenger, visiting a friend at the wheel, when he experienced his first shock of the war. As the paddle wheeler approached St. Louis, a shore battery lofted a shell that burst in front of the pilothouse. The windowed room exploded in a shower of glass, like a champagne bottle at a ship's christening.

Sam escaped undamaged except for his fix on the gloomy future. A pilothouse was a deadly place to serve in a war. "I'm not very anxious to get up into a glass perch and be shot at by either side," he wrote, and went home.

He didn't know it, but would never again take the wheel of a boat. His career on the river was over. The old steamboating days were sunk by the war. The Mississippi became a military thoroughfare.

Fearful of being pressed into service as a river pilot, he hid out at home. He found a family politely at war with itself, as was much of Missouri. His mother was as Southern as pecan pie, and her heart belonged to the Confederacy. His brother, Orion, who could almost always be counted on to make the wrong decision, admired Lincoln and backed the North. That, as it turned out, was Orion's lifelong stroke of wisdom, for the unintended consequence was to launch his brother Sam on a career as a public jester and ink-stained novelist.

Orion actively campaigned for Lincoln, whose soon-to-be attorney general, Edward Bates, was an old friend. The brand-new Territory of Nevada was in need of a secretary at $1,800 a year. Incompetency not being disqualifying, Orion got the job. The trouble was that he would have to pay his own transportation to the dusty western region. He was broke.

Sam was not. He kept rethinking his allegiances. Some days he threw in with the South, like his mother; sometimes he leaned North like his brother Orion. Neither side tempted him with great conviction. On one of his Southern days, he joined the Confederacy and marched around in the woods with his friends to get the hang of war.

Claiming with heroic fantasy to have narrowly missed being captured by a then-unknown Union officer named Ulysses S. Grant, he resigned his second lieutenant's commission. He argued that he was "incapacitated by fatigue" as a result of constant retreating. He had endured military life for some two weeks. He had done his duty to flag and Confederacy.

He hastened to join Orion on the forthcoming adventure across the wild, wild West to sagebrush Nevada. His vision of the trip had something of the innocent fever of later dime novels. He dreamed of seeing "buffaloes and Indians, and Prairie dogs, and antelopes, and may be get hanged or scalped and have ever such a fine time."

Ambling about in his spare moments, he planned on picking up gold nuggets by the pailful. He assumed that they'd be lying about as common as turnips.

He expected to return to civilization and the pilothouse in about three months. Consulting his own crystal ball, as cloudy as a bucket

Twain had visions of picking up nuggets lying about in the gold fields, as common as potatoes. All the treasure lumps needed was a light washing off.

of whitewash, he saw that by then the Civil War would have fired its last weary shot.

His prophecy was off by almost four deadly years.

Given this sublime opportunity to venture beyond the range of musket bullets, Sam put up the stiff fares for two stagecoach passages—$150 per person. He had been able to retire from the river with $800, and he took along what remained in heavy silver coins that proved to be "a good deal of a nuisance."

Arriving in St. Joseph, Missouri, the gateway to the untamed prairies, the two brothers unloaded enough luggage to burden a pack train of mules. Only then did they discover that each would be given luggage allowances of a mere twenty-five pounds. Sam's rich treasury of cuss words weighed more than that.

Compounding the baggage problem was Orion's six-pound unabridged dictionary. He insisted on taking it along, on the assumption that such a volume would be unavailable in primitive Nevada—on the outside chance that the natives spoke English at all.

Out went the white kid gloves and swallowtail coats and top hats for formal occasions. The innocent travelers sent everything home except for shirts and underclothes and a large water canteen each. At the insistence of their mother, they brought along small boxes of lemon extract to ward off scurvy.

Under a brilliant morning sky on July 26, 1861, the driver cracked the whip and gave a shout to the six fresh horses. The stagecoach quickly left "the States" in a swirl of Missouri dust. The bumpy seventeen-hundred-mile trip across the raw frontier to Carson City had begun.

The fastest way to cross the wild West was to wait until the next century . . . or to rough it for seventeen days in a stagecoach such as this. Sam Clemens roughed it and wrote a still-famous book about the adventure.

CHAPTER NINE
THE BUFFALO THAT CLIMBED A TREE

THE BROTHERS WERE WELL ARMED FOR TRAVEL through hostile terrain. With an actor's pride in his props, Sam flourished a gentle little pistol to which he was prepared to entrust his insignificant life. "I thought it was grand," he wrote of the seven-shot revolver. "It had only one fault—you could not hit anything with it."

Orion's Colt sidearm, hanging in a gunbelt, looked far more testy and comforting.

They changed horses every ten miles or so around the clock, flying across the level prairie into the sunset at 125 miles a day. The coach was loaded to the ceiling with mailbags, forcing the passengers to burrow in like moles.

They left Kansas and ventured into the western wilds of Nebraska without once having to test their weapons during Indian attack or to send back a message for a hearse. Before long Sam had set eyes for the first time on a jackrabbit. He was astonished by the creature's gross ears, almost as long as ax handles, and the hare's reserve of speed when startled. "Long after he was out of sight we could hear him whiz," Twain reported.

Sagebrush, the sequoia of the treeless desert, was something equally fresh to his Missouri eye. He found it to be a bountiful fuel for campfires, "but as a vegetable it is a distinguished failure. Nothing could abide the taste but the jackass."

Sam couldn't fail to notice that the stage drivers held the same exalted social position in the West that pilots did on the Mississippi. In the low adobe huts of the station houses where the passengers were fed and might dab a bit of water on their faces if they hurried, Twain noticed that the driver could command gourds of water. The coachman was allowed the privilege of using the station keeper's own soiled towel. Sam and Orion were obliged to dig through the ever-shifting mail sacks to find their valises and extract handkerchiefs still damp from the last stop.

With rougher terrain to conquer, the coach exchanged its horses for mules—wild beasts, in Twain's judgment. In the July heat, Sam and Orion stripped to their underwear and climbed to the roof. Tying their hats on their heads and dangling their feet over the side of the coach, they'd take in the passing scenery and marvel at the six mules flying along "as if issued from a cannon."

Still, Sam felt himself to have entered a paradise of solitude and untouched scenery and deliverance from care. The greatest human achievement to behold was the breathless glimpse of the lone and unarmed Pony Express rider, carrying mail through Indian country on his eight-day dash across eighteen hundred miles of the wild West to Sacramento.

With hearts in their parched throats, the passengers started across the dreaded quicksands of the South Platte River, notorious for gulping down whole stagecoaches, digesting passengers, and spitting out their baggage.

More than once the stagecoach's great wheels sank so quickly that Sam believed he and Orion would be drowned in the middle of the desert. But as the mails must go through, having a higher cash value than the passengers at postage of five dollars per half ounce, the six mules scrambled to safety and "sped away toward the setting sun."

The next day, facing a delay of hours while the stagecoach paused for repairs, the passengers rented horses to hunt buffaloes. It was here that Twain, ever exercising his gift for the tall tale, reported the curious event of a wild and wounded bull buffalo and the forty-foot tree.

A skyscraping tree out on the bare desert might be stretching the truth enough. But Twain was only warming up his fancy. He claimed that a fellow passenger, Bemis by name, had told him he was riding a gangly horse when charged by a wounded bison. The horse turned cartwheels in terror and bucked Bemis and saddle into the air. The immigrant went flying to the top of the lofty tree "blaspheming my luck in a way that made my breath smell of brimstone," Bemis reported.

The snorting buffalo wasn't satisfied and chose to climb the tree after him, limb by branch, higher and higher, snort by snort.

"But a bull can't climb a tree," Twain points out.

"He can't, can't he?"

The buffalo had climbed halfway to the top, astonishing the birds, only to slide back a little. "He tried again—got up a little higher . . . his eyes hot and his tongue hanging out," Bemis declared.

Twain's impractical brother, Orion Clemens, older by ten years, was clearly not burdened with a sense of humor. When Orion was appointed Secretary of Nevada Territory, Mark went along for the ride. He made the bucking stagecoach trip west famous. According to Twain, the West was so wild, cattle climbed trees.

"Higher and higher—his foot over the stump of a limb . . . getting more excited the closer he got."

From the very top of the tree, Bemis dropped a lariat, whipped out his revolver, and fired in self-defense. The buffalo stopped his ascent, reviewed the situation, gave an insolent snort, and returned to earth, too ventilated with holes ever to climb another tree.

"Bemis, is all that true, just as you have stated it?" asks Twain.

"I wish I may rot in my tracks and die the death of a dog if it isn't."

Here, as in all of his travel writings, Twain upholstered his epics with comic asides. Later he described a man shot so full of arrows "that after the Indians were gone . . . he could not restrain his tears, for his clothes were completely ruined."

Twain says little of the cuisine at the stagecoach stations, except to remark on its hazards. The Overland company featured generous slabs of rancid bacon condemned by the U.S. Army and bought at bargain rates. "Our breakfast was before us, but our teeth were idle," as Twain expressed it.

Venturing into Rocky Mountain country, they were confronted with barely civilized table companions. Here, a man without a price on his head was considered a slow learner in the outlaw and desperado trade. The most feared of them all was a legendary killer named Slade, with a temper like a rattrap. Slade. Just Slade.

Sitting down to breakfast one morning, Twain found a quiet and affable gentlemen at his elbow. "Never youth stared and shivered as I did when I heard them call him SLADE!"

Slade! The man who had killed twenty-six men!

Twain recalled, "The coffee ran out. At least it was reduced to one tin cupful, and Slade was about to take it when he saw that my cup was empty. He politely offered to fill it, but although I wanted it, I politely declined. I was afraid he had not killed anybody that morning, and might be seeking a diversion. But still with firm politeness he insisted on filling my cup. . . ."

Young Sam drank it and waited for the pistol shot ending his unpromising career. Instead, like a gentleman, the great desperado accompanied him out to the coach waiting to go charging up the Rockies.

Chapter Ten
THIEVES, MURDERERS, AND DESPERADOES

T HE MISSOURI BOYS TRAVELED A SWEATY 798 stagecoach miles before they stopped for a bath, whether they attracted flies or not. The creaking Concord coach didn't normally halt for such Eastern niceties and time wasters.

Now, like a mountain goat, the coach began the struggle up the Rockies into perpetual snows. Sam's eye could make out relics of the California Gold Rush a decade earlier: the phosphorescent ribs of mules and horses, glowing in the night. Sheets of rain caught the travelers, revealing that the coach leaked from every pore and crevice. The river baths down below were now repeated, lacking only bars of soap.

At last the coach rolled into Salt Lake City. Sam and Orion had a restaurant supper, unpacked, and slept two nights in hotel beds, spared the mail sacks as companions.

With six hundred scenic miles yet to travel, they found room in the coach for boiled ham and hard-boiled eggs. Once again, the driver cracked his whip and they shot off.

As Twain was to recall, "Nothing helps scenery like ham and eggs."

But ahead blazed a sunlit death sentence—sixty-eight unbroken miles across the man-eating Great Salt Lake Desert, a carnivore with notoriously bad table manners. Recalled Twain, "The sun beat down with dead, blistering, relentless malignity . . . there is not a merciful shred of cloud in all the brilliant firmament; there is not a living creature visible in any direction . . . not a sound—not a sigh—not a whisper—not a buzz or a whir of wings, or distant pipe of bird—not even a sob from the lost souls . . . making one feel more lonesome and forsaken than before."

Sam's water canteen, and Orion's, went dry before they emerged from the "concentrated hideousness" to safety at last. Twain recalled that they were glad to have the bulky dictionary along, "because we never could have found language to tell how glad we were, in any sort of dictionary but an unabridged one."

In mid-August, on the twentieth day of their journey, Sam and his brother, shedding clouds of white alkali dust, stepped from the coach into new lives. They had reached their destination at last: Carson City, Nevada Territory.

Not a tree stood in sight, although a flagpole shot up like a Roman candle in the center of the plaza. This capital city of Nevada, population 2,000, had garlands of sagebrush and greasewood growing along the side streets. "It never rains here and the dew never falls," Twain noted. "The birds that fly over the land carry their own provisions with them."

The brothers moved into a rooming house at ten dollars a week, each. As private secretary to the exalted secretary of the territory, Sam had nothing to do and, accordingly, was being paid nothing. He was free for sightseeing, if he could find any sights but horned toads and tumbleweeds.

The glorious citizenry, on the other hand, exceeded his expectations: "Thieves, murderers, desperadoes, ladies, children, lawyers, Christians, Indians, Chinamen, Spaniards, gamblers, sharpers, coyotes . . . poets, preachers, and jackass rabbits" milled about in the streets. The Territory was not going to be dull. In lawless Aurora, to the south, the city marshal reported, "All quiet. . . . Five men will be hung in an hour."

It could never have occurred to Sam that he would be moved to write about his trip west, for he took no notes. But Orion, as a state official, apparently felt obliged to. It was eleven years later that Twain stuck a cigar between his teeth and began scribbling away. He would publish his adventures in a humorous patchwork he called *Roughing It.*

Orion's notes aside, preoccupied as they were with weather and distances traveled each day, one sees the leechlike memory for fine detail of a Mississippi river pilot. Here, at random, is the precision of his observation and his total recall of the rattle-boned coyote of the West.

He has a general slinking expression all over. The coyote is a living, breathing allegory of Want. He is *always* Hungry. He is always poor, out of luck and friendless. The meanest creatures despise him, and even the fleas would desert him for a velocipede [bicycle]. He is so spiritless and cowardly that even while his exposed teeth are pretending a threat, the rest of his face is apologizing for it. And he is so homely!— so scrawny, and ribby, and coarse-haired, and pitiful. . . .

We soon learned to recognize the sharp, vicious bark of the coyote as it came across the murky plain at night to disturb our dreams among the mail sacks.

Before long, the family curse gripped Sam once more. Like his father with his doomed silkworms, the young Clemens paused to gaze at the hundred-foot pine trees as thick as fur on the surrounding mountains. A magnificent get-rich-quick notion struck him. He'd become a mountain baron.

The boom towns below, Carson City and Virginia City, were eating lumber for breakfast. He'd establish a claim, free of charge, to a princely parcel of trees around Lake Tahoe and harvest the timber. This would beat growing coca at the headwaters of the Amazon River, and the climate was better.

The scheme might have worked, except that Sam got absentminded about his breakfast fire. Unattended, it leaped free. By the time the lumber baron smelled smoke, an entire side of the mountain was

A flattering portrait of a man named Will Stewart, one of the social elite of Nevada Territory, a boisterous friend of Sam's who went on to become a senator of the new state.

Clemens had never seen a coyote before. Neither had the Connecticut illustrator, True Williams. This scavenger looks too well-fed and conceited.

crackling up in flames. Sam's entire inventory of pines was vanishing before his eyes. His dream of riches lay in smoke and hot ashes.

He climbed down the mountainside to civilization on the alkali flats. His sense of humor left home for a while. Finally he shrugged off the tragedy and resumed an aimless life. He might have taken another claim on mountain pines, but that get-rich scheme was too inflammable. Something fireproof might turn up.

Something did. It came on the wind.

Every afternoon at two o'clock, dusty gale winds swept through Carson City, rolling up tin roofs "like sheet music."

The citizens spent the afternoons chasing their hats.

But even stronger winds from the nearby Humboldt County mountains were sweeping the town. Rumors, some of them true, of men going to bed poor as dirt and awakening millionaires caught Sam's gloomy attention. The mountains were believed to be stuffed like jewelry stores with gold and silver. His dream came alive again and he became as "frenzied as the craziest."

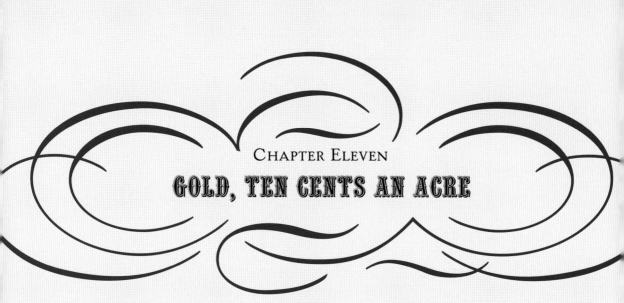

CHAPTER ELEVEN
GOLD, TEN CENTS AN ACRE

"HURRY, WAS THE WORD!" TWAIN WROTE AS HE and three equally frenzied friends set out in early winter for the fabled Comstock lode in get-rich-quick Humboldt County. There raw, prehistoric silver had once flowed like lava. Any moment, the treasure might be dug up and all carted away.

During a slow and laborious trek north, the travelers hastened their pace only when chased by a pack of wolves. The men reached their destination in a howling snowstorm. With great foresight, they had brought along fourteen decks of playing cards to enjoy their rest from the stoop labor of picking up nuggets of gold and polished bricks of silver.

"I confess, without shame, that I expected to find masses of silver lying all about the ground," Twain later wrote. "I expected to see it glittering in the sun on the mountain summits."

Almost at once, he did catch sight of a promising glitter of sparks in a granite-rich riverbed. Within a week or two, he now convinced himself, Samuel L. Clemens would be inexhaustibly wealthy. He began castle-building plans to spend his fortune.

But when his specimen underwent examination by wiser eyes, it was declared to be "granite rubbish and nasty glittering mica that isn't worth ten cents an acre!" Samuel L. Clemens had rediscovered fool's gold.

Like bloodhounds casting for the scent of treasure, Sam and his friends tramped through miles of hardscrabble terrain. Miracle of miracles, they stumbled across a ledge with a trace of silver and staked a claim, naming it "the Monarch of the Mountains."

They quickly learned it would be necessary to sink a shaft down hundreds of feet to follow the trace to its kingdom of silver. Undaunted, Sam joined in with pick and shovel, crowbar and blasting powder.

"One week of this satisfied me," wrote Twain. "I resigned."

His friends soon followed. The Monarch's fiefdom was demoted to a mere hole in the ground and abandoned to the coyotes.

His return on the road to Carson City was a black comedy,

Twain was caught in a blizzard so cold it froze everything but his sense of humor.

providing laughter for anyone not cast as its principal player. Here Sam miscalculated, for he was the principal player.

When a blinding snowstorm came howling in, Sam and his intrepid party soon resigned themselves to freezing to death. Their matches had blown out in the bitter night wind, and attempts to start a fire by shooting into kindling had failed. Sam felt he might as well abandon his bad habits, and threw away his beloved pipe. He'd be frozen stiff by morning, anyway.

When he was soon awakened, to discover he lay a mere fifteen feet in the dark from the stagecoach inn, he jumped up and went looking in the snowbanks for his pipe.

It was as close as he was to come to taking harp lessons in the hereafter. Said he, "The whole situation was so painfully ridiculous and humiliating" that he was unable to summon up his usual wit for the occasion. Years later, he would attest, perhaps from this early visit, that there was no laughter in Heaven.

Nothing was wasted on the Missouri tenderfoot. He had formerly found it diverting on occasion to convert his personal travail into humorous pieces for newspapers. He would soon go at it seriously, shaking laughter out of his ragged sleeves.

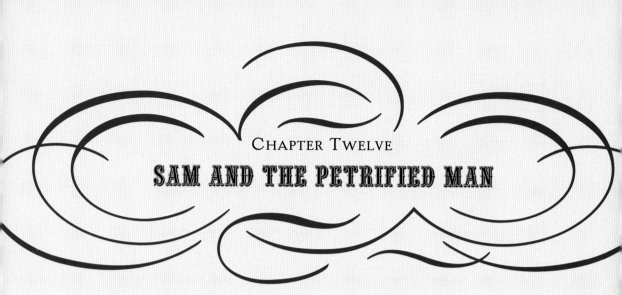

CHAPTER TWELVE

SAM AND THE PETRIFIED MAN

AM WENT BROKE. BY 1862, THE DIGGINGS HAD snatched away the last of his riverboat hoard of coins. He woke up one July morning, a pauper at age twenty-six.

He had written a burlesque about a lecturer so full of himself that it was "impossible to print his lecture in full, as the typecases had run out of capital i's." The sketch found its way to Virginia City, where it caught the eye of Joe Goodman, whimsical editor of the *Daily Territorial Enterprise*. One of the few Jews in the Territory, he could detect talent in its wet-behind-the-ears stage. He offered Sam a reporter's job at twenty-five dollars a week.

Despite a failure of his past dreams, Twain continued running a prospector's fever. He thought it would be foolish to retreat, when

Mark Twain walked through these doors of the *Territorial Enterprise's* knockabout newspaper office and print shop in Virginia City. Here he unearthed the notorious petrified man.

the next mountain might be shot through with gold and silver. But looking at himself, he saw a fly-specked daguerreotype of a miner down on his luck. How shabby had the riverboat dandy become, with even his bushy eyebrows caked white with alkali dust. Reviewing his career to date promised only that he would become a distinguished failure.

"I had been a grocery clerk, for one day," he recalled. But he had eaten so much candy, the proprietor had fired him. "I studied law for an entire week," he added, only to give it up as boring. He failed at blacksmithing and took a job as a "bookseller's clerk for a while, but the customers bothered me so much I could not read with any comfort, and so the proprietor gave me a furlough and forgot to put a limit on it."

Joy was not the raw material of humor, Twain was to discover. The dark source was sorrow. In his hands, as he recalled the bruises of his past, sorrow often wore slap shoes and a putty nose.

He accepted the newspaper offer. Unable to afford coach travel, he claims to have hiked the 130 miles to Virginia City. There he began his career as a professional writer and resident wit.

Inside the editorial office he saw that the editors, reporters, and even the printers carried revolvers. Wrangling words and sentences in the prickly Territory evidently made one nervous. It was public knowledge that the first twenty-six corpses in the brand-new cemetery had arrived shot through with bullet holes of various calibers.

Newspaper humor was the soothing aspirin of the day. Life was especially testy and unpleasant in Nevada, where one might as well be trying to scratch out a living on the moon. Civilization had not yet embraced show business with radio, television, movies, computers, and cell phones. Goodman of the *Enterprise* felt obliged to relieve public boredom and distress with his unruly daily newspaper. Clemens was turned loose on Virginia City to find news to print, whether it was fit or not.

The newly minted reporter encountered difficulties. The thoroughfares were laid out one way, with no cross streets. You needed a stagecoach to go around the block. And ambling about town to question the citizens for news, he found that "nobody knew anything."

With newspaper space to fill, he regarded a shooting down the street as a divine and timely gift. He filled two joyous columns.

But soon the greatest excitement in town might be the arrival of a hay wagon. He knew from his Missouri days setting type that "stirring news" was the soul of a newspaper, and he decided to kick up some mischief. There was, after all, a competing newspaper in town, the thin-skinned *Union*.

Sam gave his bubbling imagination a stir and ladled out a wondrous hoax. He reported the discovery of a petrified man.

Dipping a pen in ink, he served up the sorrowful details: The stone man had a wooden leg; he'd been found in a sitting position with a "pensive" expression on his dead face. Samuel L. Clemens would have a newspaper scoop.

Of course, nobody would believe the journalistic horseplay, especially when pausing at Sam's precise description of the relic's right thumb and fingers in relationship to its hundred-year-old profile. Nevertheless, the *Enterprise*'s boomtown readers would be stirred to laughter. And the *Union* could be counted on for a fit of jealousy at the *Enterprise*'s journalistic drollery.

The hoax was picked up by newspapers across the country and it made a great stir. To Sam's immense surprise, the petrified man was accepted as genuine. Few readers had troubled to unravel the young author's detailed description of the gent's right hand. They would

The well-dressed journalist wore boots and a pistol.

The young publisher and free spirit of the *Territorial Enterprise*, Joe Goodman. Later, he would write a scholarly book on Maya hieroglyphics.

The first twenty-six corpses buried in Virginia City's new cemetery arrived leaking from fresh bullet holes.

have discovered that the petrified man, fingers aflutter, had his thumb at his nose in a universal gesture of playful contempt.

At the same time, Clemens reacted with dismay at the gross humbugability of his fellow man. This judgment would agitate his sensibilities until he petrified into a public scold. So ruffled did he become at the human gift for homespun ignorance and hypocrisy, for greed and crackpot bigotry, that he would become a one-man firing squad.

"Our Heavenly Father invented man because he was disappointed in the monkey," he declared.

"If you pick up a starving dog and make him prosperous, he will not bite you. That is the principal difference between a dog and a man."

"April I. This is the day upon which we are reminded of what we are on the other three hundred and sixty-four."

Meanwhile, Sam kept a gleeful eye on rowdy Virginia City, as if viewing it through a microscope distorted by a cracked lens. He saw what he chose to see. He took a newspaperman's delight in the city's upstanding desperadoes: Sugarfoot Mike, Pock-Marked Jake, El Dorado Johnny, and Six-Fingered Pete. Sam's study of mankind, begun on the Mississippi River, was continuing here, powdered over with alkali dust.

Within two years on the *Enterprise*, Clemens had turned himself inside out. He'd arrived as a self-assured but disheveled novice, whose only commitment was to making heaps of money. By 1864, he was a skilled and gilded journalist who could forge phrases like no one else on the scene, and who had a talent for spring-loading his sentences with laughter.

And then he forgot that he couldn't shoot straight. He challenged a fellow newspaperman to a duel.

Chapter Thirteen
The Duel at Dawn

ENTER FEARLESS, FIDDLE-PLAYING STEVE GILLIS. He was a flyspeck of a newspaper typesetter and street fighter weighing in at ninety-five pounds after a heavy meal. He had a taste for elaborate jokes and general deviltries. When Sam and the rival editor of the *Union* began insulting each other in newsprint, Gillis urged his "pard" to take action—nothing less than to challenge the pompous rascal across town to a genuine duel of pistols. Virginia City's code of honor, so brief it could be written on a grain of rice, demanded action.

Sam shrugged off the opportunity to grow wings so early in the day. But James Laird, the rival editor, published further charges, the least of which stated that Clemens was "a liar, a poltroon, and a puppy." Poltroon was an elegant way of saying that Sam was a contemptible coward.

The Missouri mischief maker exploded. With Gillis holding his coat, Sam supervised the wording of a formal challenge and sent it over to the *Union*.

Sam was emboldened to learn that his friend Gillis was a veteran of many duels, "but of the impromptu kind." Even their boss, Joe Goodman, had lost a lock of hair in a duel and lived to tell about it. But Sam made out his will anyway, and hardly managed a wink of sleep.

The civic event was scheduled for dawn. Gillis would be Sam's second. They stumbled to a nearby ravine a couple of hours early so that Clemens could get in a little target practice. They set up a fence rail for Sam to sharpen his aim.

Gillis called out, "One . . . two . . . three . . ."

Sam shut his eyes and pulled the trigger. The rail remained untouched and defiant. Recalling the event years later, Gillis picks up the story.

Just then we heard somebody shooting over in the next ravine.

Sam asked: "What's that, Steve?"

"Why," I said, "that's Laird. His seconds are practicing him over there."

It didn't make my principal any more cheerful to hear that pistol go off every few seconds. . . .

The movement of a mudhen off in the sagebrush caught Gillis's eye.

Gillis said, "Let me have that pistol. I'll show you how to shoot."

He handed it to me, and I let go at the bird and shot its head off, clean. About that time Laird and his second came over the ridge to meet us. I saw them coming and handed [Sam] back the pistol. We were looking at the bird when they came up.

"Who did that?" asked Laird's second.

"Sam," I said.

"How far off was it?"

"Oh, about thirty yards."

"Can he do it again?"

"Of course. Every time. He could do it twice that far."

Had Mark Twain not survived the duel with a rival newspaper editor, this might have been his last photograph. It was about this time that he looked in a mirror and abandoned the side whiskers. He discovered that he was photogenic, and for the rest of his life he was never known to pass a camera without stopping to strike a pose.

Laird conferred with his second and decided a duel with Clemens would land him an obituary notice in both papers. Would Sam agree to settle the matter privately, with apologies all around?

It was done.

But the matter was far from finished, and Clemens soon would be obliged to leave a forwarding address—in haste.

An impatient new law had come down that made dueling a penitentiary crime, for both principal and second. Clemens and Gillis were warned that they had only hours to get out of town, and they caught the morning stagecoach to San Francisco.

Chapter Fourteen
SAM IN THE BIG CITY

AM WAS GLAD TO GET THE ALKALI DUST OUT OF his nostrils. He was quite ready for the change to San Francisco's lamplit streets and starched-shirt entertainments. At the same time, he was sorry to abandon the abrasive, windblown city that had provided him with the merriest days of his life. He carried with him a hen's nest of paper shares in mining stocks, gorgeously engraved, that needed only a little more cackling and setting time to hatch.

Staying in the best hotel, the Occidental, he and Gillis descended on San Francisco like heirs to a great fortune. They embraced the six theaters and shed silver dollars like wet dogs shaking themselves dry. In evening dress, young Sam danced the evenings away "with a step peculiar to myself—and the kangaroo."

But once again Sam's confidence in mining shares proved fanciful. The bottom fell out of his Nevada hole in the ground. He woke up one morning wiped out. His stock certificates were of value only as bunkhouse wallpaper. He was, once again, a pauper.

While Sam may have been the literary tiger of Virginia City, he discovered that he was only a homeless alley cat in San Francisco. After a round of the newspaper offices, he and Gillis were obliged to settle for the grubbiest daily in town, the *Morning Call*. With a subscription price of twelve and one-half cents a week, the cheapest in town, it appealed to the poor and was dismissed as "the washerwoman's paper." Worse, the *Call* was comfortably bigoted.

Twain's collision with his youthful race prejudice had not yet made a public noise. That would come later, with a complete repudiation of his past racism as he brought to life the runaway slave Jim in the pages of *Huckleberry Finn*. But a rehearsal event was waiting for him at his big city job.

In addition to the paper's social denseness, Clemens felt in the wrong harness at the fact-obsessed *Call*. His nimble imagination went unappreciated. He was heavily blue penciled for writing sentences his editor regarded as salty caviar to the paper's

Among the social graces, Twain tried dancing, but he was more talented at swearing.

Twain "raked" these early San Francisco streets for news, and found bigotry and corruption in abundance.

meat-and-potato readers. Sam's days, ten and twelve hours long, became drudgery.

While at the *Call*, he witnessed an incident that refreshed his memory of man's passion for cruelty. While "raking" the town from end to end for news, he came upon a street scene in which Irish immigrants had assaulted and set their dogs on a Chinese laundryman in an unprovoked attack. A policeman looked on with profound disinterest, if not amusement.

Clemens wrote up the assault "with considerable warmth and holy indignation." He attacked the police force for its racism. It was hardly a revelation to him that the Irish and the Chinese were in combat for the lowest rung on the social ladder, but injustice was not a trifle. He was dumbfounded when the editor refused to publish the piece. Chinese didn't subscribe to the *Call*. The Irish did.

Already weary of his adventures in lowbrow journalism, Clemens resigned from the paper. He did this with the full encouragement and relief of the editor, who clearly saw that Sam Clemens had no future in the journalist's trade.

Clemens never forgot the editor's insult to his pride. Nor did he forgive the paper's mean-spirited pandering to the prejudices of its readers. What was a newspaper without compassion? Forty-odd years later, white haired and white suited, he took pleasure when the great San Francisco earthquake of 1906 struck the *Call* building, leaving only a collapse of bricks, revealing no backbone.

Like an active volcano, Twain erupted from time to time about his favorite villain. "All I care to know is that a man is a human being—that is enough for me; he can't be any worse."

"Concerning the difference between man and the jackass: Some observers hold that there isn't any. But that wrongs the jackass."

Broke again, he moved again—five times in four months.

CHAPTER FIFTEEN
THE SLOUCHING MAN

Now, in September of 1864, Clemens couldn't have escaped battlefield events of the Civil War. News was reaching San Francisco in clusters of dots and dashes, by telegraph. General William Tecumseh Sherman had set Atlanta afire and begun his historic March to the Sea, burning a path through the rebellious South.

Except for a couple of asides, the war is conspicuously absent in Twain's autobiography. One can understand a certain mortification he might have felt, pen in hand, for having slyly fled the Confederacy after treating his two weeks of service as a parlor joke. To make matters worse, he had warmed to the North, and years later he would embrace General Ulysses S. Grant as a devoted friend and hero.

While unemployed, Clemens did briefly consider a return to the Mississippi River to pursue his former career. He would surely be able to serve as a military river pilot for the North. He seemed to pursue inertia instead.

"Mark was the laziest man I ever knew in my life," Steve Gillis was to say late in life, with a qualification. "Mentally, he was the hardest worker I ever knew." Gillis couldn't recall his old pardner without a book in hand, in a plucky resolve to continue his education. With a history of France or England, Sam would prop himself up in bed and read until the book slipped from his hands.

If we are to accept his own anguished words, for two months Clemens was a tragic pauper. "I became a very adept at 'slinking,'" he said. "I slunk from back street to back street, I slunk away from approaching faces that looked familiar. I slunk to my meals. . . . I slunk to my bed. . . . I felt more despicable than the worms. During all this time I had but one piece of money—a silver ten-cent piece—and held to it and would not spend it on any account, lest the consciousness coming strong upon me that I was entirely penniless, might suggest suicide. I had pawned everything but the clothes I had on: So I clung to my dime desperately, till it was smooth with handling."

He dodged his friends so well that no witnesses survived to confirm his adventure in poverty. The tale may be an exhibit of his playful remark to "Get your facts first, and then you can distort them as much as you please."

At any rate, his last dime has never turned up. He was, in fact, writing essays at the time for a San Francisco magazine calling itself *The Californian*. The editor paid him twelve dollars for each piece, a bountiful sum in those days.

The editor was pockmarked but handsome Bret Harte, soon to become briefly more famous than Twain himself. Today, after almost 150 years, Harte's Gold Rush tales, such as *Outcasts of Poker Flat* and *The Luck of Roaring Camp*, are still read.

San Francisco's two proudest literary figures became close friends, and Twain credited Harte with valuable editorial help. But the friendship headed onto the rocks. In an 1878 letter to the editor and writer William Dean Howells, Twain catalogs Harte's grating frailties, including his attempt to conceal his Jewish birth. Twain had had enough of Harte's ever-inflating ego, his airy indifference to the feelings of others, and his hobby of sponging off his friends, including Sam himself.

When Twain slouched in despair, he made a three-act drama out of it.

The fashion plate of the California gold rush. Bret Harte, writer and editor, became a brighter celebrity than Twain, but his wattage quickly dimmed.

Following his fanciful adventure in poverty, Clemens began writing a daily San Francisco column for his old friend Joe Goodman at the Virginia City *Enterprise*. Once again, Sam was able to support himself in the carefree, bohemian style that amused him. He regarded life that centered around the distinguished Occidental Hotel as "Heaven on the half-shell."

Through the years he had much to say about shelters, leaving behind Twainisms like room tips. He recalled a hotel with partitions so thin one could hear "occupants of adjoining rooms changing their minds." Of another inn, he noted that it "used to be a good hotel, but that proves nothing—I used to be a good boy."

He was not moved to similar quips about the rudeness of the local city fathers when they pulled the welcome mat out from under his feet. In his daily column, he had been writing a scorching exposé of crooked politicians and police corruption among the foggy hills of San Francisco. The chief of police filed a libel suit and rattled handcuffs.

At the same time, Sam's bantam sidekick, feisty Steve Gillis, had gotten into a barroom fight and put his adversary in the hospital. Arrested and charged with assault, Gillis would be facing a murder charge if the patient chose to die. Sam posted bail of $500. Once out of jail, Gillis jumped bail. He grabbed his fiddle and lit out of town for the hills. Clemens evidently decided that he, too, should be somewhere else, and went with him. The heat would die down. San Francisco was too devoted to moneymaking to hold a grudge.

Drawing on such youthful dismay at the greed and sleaze of the political class, Twain later forged a comic remark heard around the world. "Suppose you were an idiot," he wrote. "And suppose you were a member of Congress. But I repeat myself."

The two newspapermen hid out in a place called Jackass Hill. You'd think Clemens had coined the name himself.

CHAPTER SIXTEEN

THE TALKING BLUEJAY

FINDING HIMSELF IN OLD MINING COUNTRY, Clemens once again was overcome by a cunning old malady—intermittent gold fever. He began scratching around in the dirt and hoped this time Lady Luck might toss a few nuggets at his feet. She lurked around these hills, didn't she?

This time, he covered his bet. While he'd once been driven by dreams of fame and fortune, he'd now settle for fame. He began filling pages of a notebook with possible story material.

Jackass Hill was a chaparral-covered Swiss cheese. Earlier prospectors had left holes behind like gophers. Sam listened to local tales of miners who, in a single shovel-load of earth, washed out $500 in gold. Or $1,000. Nearby, a pocket of the yellow stuff had yielded $60,000. Clemens would return to the shovel, the pickax, and the dream.

But the glory days of the hill and the gulch were long gone to cobwebs. A population of two or three thousand, by Twain's reckoning, had wasted away to a wide scattering of some twenty dogged scavengers. Six ramshackle cabins stood like tombstones over the grassy hillsides and amid the live oaks.

Clemens could hardly have chosen a more congenial abode. The cabin, owned by Steve Gillis's brother Jim, had a feast of books to satisfy Sam's raging appetite. Here were the plays of Shakespeare, the novels of Dickens, the poetry of Lord Byron, and the philosophy of Francis Bacon. On rainy days, Sam took up residence next to the log fire and gorged.

His host, Jim Gillis, could read Greek and Latin, and no doubt curse in them as well. Bearded, shabby, and callused from eighteen years of largely luckless prospecting, he'd been educated in medicine, and knew his way around leeches and castor oil. Instead of hanging out his shingle, Jim had pursued a fantasy that left him pleasantly exiled on Jackass Hill. His newspapering brother Steve was not afflicted with fantasies. Steve abandoned

The Jim Gillis cabin, where Mark wrote the first rough draft of the jumping frog story.

The same cabin, fancifully restored. What happened to the windows?

the cabin and took off for his old typesetting job on the Virginia City *Enterprise*.

Clemens quickly discovered that his host was a storyteller with a humble, underplayed sense of humor. Sam made detailed notes. He responded to the music of vernacular speech, which was to become his own literary language.

And finally, at long last, a benign madness came over Sam: He felt tempted to become a genuine professional writer, a respected literary man like his San Francisco pockmarked friend Bret Harte.

It was here, at the cabin's log fire, that Jim's talent met Sam's late-blooming genius. Out would fly the only bluejay in world literature—a rara avis speaking the greatest one-liners written for a bird since those of the ancient Greek playwright Aristophanes.

Never in a hurry, Twain would let years pass before he dug out his old Jackass Hill notes and set Gillis's tale to his own music. He made the hero of the story Gillis himself, who soberly claimed to have mastered the art of talking to animals. Shielding his retiring friend from public notice, Sam changed Gillis's name. He called the piece "Jim Baker's Bluejay Yarn."

Here, in a sample, is Twain at work.

According to Jim Baker, some animals have only a limited education, and use only simple words. . . . whereas certain other animals have a large vocabulary, a fine command of language, and a ready and fluent delivery . . . and they enjoy "showing off."

The best talker, according to Baker after long observations, is the bluejay.

He has got more moods, and more different kinds of feelings than other creatures; and mind you, whatever a bluejay feels he can put into language. And no mere commonplace language, either, but rattling, out-and-out book-talk—and bristling with metaphor, too—just bristling! And for command of language—why you never see a bluejay get stuck for a word. . . . They just boil out of him! . . . And another thing . . . there's no bird, or cow or anything that uses as good grammar as a bluejay. . . . Well, a cat does—but you let a cat get excited, once; you let a cat get to pulling fur with another on a shed, nights, and you'll hear grammar that'll give you the lockjaw. . . .

You may call a jay a bird. Well, so he is, in a measure—because he's got feathers on him, and don't belong to no church, perhaps; but otherwise he is just as much a human as you be. . . . A jay hasn't got any more principle than a congressman. A jay will lie, a jay will steal, a jay will deceive, a jay will betray. . . .

Now on top of all that, there's another thing: a jay can outswear any gentleman in the mines. You think a cat can swear. Well, a cat can; but give a bluejay a subject that calls for his reserve powers . . . yes, sir, a jay is everything a man is. . . . A jay can reason and plan and discuss. . . . If a jay ain't human, he better take in his sign, that's all.

After this sermon on natural history, Twain launches "the little incident" that had happened a few years earlier. A bluejay with an acorn in its mouth landed on the roof of an abandoned cabin across the way. The bird started up a conversation with Jim, causing the acorn to fall from its beak and through a knothole in the roof.

But he can't hear the acorn strike bottom. "Why didn't I hear it fall!" the jaybird wails, putting his eye to the hole and peering down as far as his eye can see. "Must be a mighty long hole."

Continues the witness to all this, "So he flew off and fetched another acorn and dropped it in, and tried to flirt his eye to the hole quick enough to see what became of it, but he was too late. . . . 'Confound it, I don't seem to understand this thing, no way; however I'll tackle her again,'" he overhears the bluejay remark.

Again and again, the bluejay returns to drop acorns down the knothole and peer after them. Finally, he says to Jim in perfect English, "I've shoveled acorns enough in there to keep the family thirty years, and if I can see a sign of one of 'em I wish I may land in a museum with a belly full of sawdust."

Soon other bluejays stop by to have a look and discuss the mystery. One of them slips through the doorway into the abandoned cabin. "He flopped his wing and raised a whoop. 'Come here!' he says. 'Come here, everybody; hang'd if this fool hasn't been trying to fill up a house with acorns!'"

This story did not make Twain famous—he was already famous when he got around to writing it. He himself, not a talking bluejay, was about to drop a tale down the public chimney that would land with a bang.

CHAPTER SEVENTEEN
THE WATER BOY FROM JACKASS HILL

THE ONLY WINGED RESIDENTS OF THE GOLD-MINING town of celestial Angel's Camp were horseflies and mosquitoes. The rough-hewn village was named after the surprised miner, Henry Angel, who first panned flakes of gold out of the creek.

When Clemens discovered the place, over in Calaveras County, California, it was "snoring like a steamboat." The excitement was gone. But who knew what patch of earth had escaped the prospectors' frenzies?

The new arrivals had no luck around Jackass Gulch, where Clemens and Jim Gillis had "panned up and down the hillsides till they looked plowed like a field; we could have put in a crop of grain."

The prospectors tramped over to Angel's Camp, only to find themselves mired in mud and stung by whipsaws of rain.

They took cover in a dilapidated tavern. Dozing over by the stove was a man who would make history in Clemens's career. He was Ben Coon, a former Illinois River pilot and barroom boor. He was slow in speech and given to telling endless stories with all the charm and gusto of a funeral oration.

But Clemens found himself not only listening but taking notes about the jumping frog contest once formerly staged in a clearing in Calaveras County. The bare bones of the drama had been around the camps, but Sam had never heard the tale before.

Except for notes to remind him, he might have forgotten the backwoods sonnet when a new and unfamiliar event captured his attention. Pay dirt turned up—at last!

The two prospectors may have clicked their heels and done a little dance. Probably.

The more experienced Jim Gillis began working the hillside prospects. Sam carried up pails of water to wash out the gold dust from the pans of fresh earth. Gillis was following the "color" to what they hoped would disclose a blinding bonanza of treasure.

After several days of hoisting water pails through the mud and icy rain, the work lost its fascination for Sam. He was wet down to his skin. He was shivering. His teeth were chattering as if he had a mouthful of castanets. And it was beginning to snow.

"Jim," he said. "I won't carry any more water. This work is too disagreeable."

"Just one more pail, Sam," Jim pleaded.

"No, sir, not a drop, not if I knew there were a million dollars in that pan."

The philosophical Gillis gave in. They could get rich another day.

To protect their discovery, Gillis posted a handwritten note, staking a claim to the remote spot for thirty days, by miner's law. Dodging pneumonia, they fled the January rains to wait out the weather seven miles away in Angel's Camp.

Not long before, Sam had reached his twenty-ninth birthday. What had he now to show for his many labors: a shallow hole and a small pile of dirt with a note of ownership stuck in it. What a depressing achievement for a man who had read Shakespeare and could navigate a French sentence without getting lost.

Twain quickly abandoned his career as a beast of burden in the diggings. Instead of nuggets, he picked up a pen.

His experiences in the Wild West bucked Twain into worldwide fame as a rebel with a gift for laughter.

Sam soon took cover in Gillis's cabin on Jackass Hill, there to linger by the log fire.

He passed the time with the jumping frog epic, getting a clumsy first draft on paper. He was not happy with it. Maybe he'd credit it to that fanciful nobody, Mark Twain.

In due time, the snow melted and the rains passed, but not before showering away the earth covering the Gillis-Clemens claim. Voilà! A nest of yellow nuggets now lay freshly washed in the sunlight. Pure gold!

Unfortunately, the rains had also washed in two undaunted Austrian miners, who had observed the gold and the staked notice. They camped on the spot to wait out the expiration of the thirty-day limit. When no one showed up, they claimed the spot for themselves and were believed to have dug up a fortune.

That was enough mining for Sam. He lit out for San Francisco with the pages of the jumping frog story rolled up in his pocket.

Chapter Eighteen

Good-Bye, Sam; Hello, Mark

CLEMENS AGAIN CAMPED OUT IN TEMPORARY splendor in the Occidental Hotel on Montgomery Street. With telegraph poles standing like toothpicks across the country, San Francisco was getting its news as fresh as oysters and petrale sole from the bay. The Civil War ended. The actor John Wilkes Booth shot Abraham Lincoln. And slavery would soon end with passage of the Thirteenth Amendment to the Constitution.

How Twain reacted to all these stunning events is unknown; his autobiography is silent. But then, he chose his materials carefully. What was too grave to allow him to hoist a laugh, he was apt to bury. Like most artists, he played to his strengths.

He sat at the window of his hotel room and twice more rewrote

Telegraph poles had reached San Francisco, bringing news from afar and perches for seagulls. Soon Twain himself would be making a noise, and the news would travel in the other direction.

the frog tale. He was having a structural problem and the voice of the story needed retuning. Eventually he got all the elements airborne, like a juggling trick. He christened the piece "Jim Smiley and His Jumping Frog," but he tried on names like hats and finally the tale came to be known as "The Celebrated Jumping Frog of Calaveras County."

The frog began to exercise its legs well before publication. Clemens—now Twain—sent the amphibian to his literary friend Artemus Ward, who was editing a collection of Nevada sketches. But the story reached New York too late to slip between the book covers. Given a prod by the publisher, the frog leaped to a weekly magazine, the *Saturday Press*, rising from the ashes of the Civil War. The story hit the East on November 18, 1865. At age thirty, Mark Twain caught a shooting star in his bare hands.

"The sketch scored a direct hit on the American postwar funny bone," wrote the Twain scholar Ron Powers. The comedy raced back across the country, coming to rest in the pages of Bret Harte's *Californian*.

San Francisco awoke to discover that a great humorist had been living among them under another name. Mark Twain was toasted

The young author at hard labor, searching for a word. The difference between the right word and the almost right word was "the difference between lightning and the lightning bug," he said.

In San Francisco, Twain regretfully parted from Sammy Clemens. Even his friends began to call him Mark.

and celebrated. Any handcuff rattling by the chief of police irked by old slanders was forgotten—if, indeed, the story of Sam's abandoning town ahead of the police was entirely true.

But honors and handshakes didn't pay the rent. Sam resumed writing daily San Francisco pieces for Joe Goodman's Virginia City newspaper at twenty-five dollars a week. And again he raised his literary slingshot at police corruption and shadowy politics.

At the same time, Mark Twain was giving a hug and waving good-bye to his boyhood friend, Samuel L. Clemens.

CHAPTER NINETEEN
THE SANDWICH CHRONICLES

ARK SAW A DAZZLING NEW STEAMSHIP, THE *Ajax*, returning from a voyage to the exotic Sandwich Islands, and he packed his bag for the next trip. The *what* islands?

Captain James Cook, the English voyager who put the Pacific Ocean on the map, had discovered a clutch of paradise islands and named them after his friend in the British admiralty, Lord Sandwich. No stranger to fame, the good lord had already bestowed upon civilization the sandwich, virtually making silverware obsolete.

Mark had arranged with newspaper friends at the *Sacramento Union* to write a series of letters, or articles, about the tropical ports of call that we know today as the Hawaiian Islands.

In the tropical heat of Hawaii, then known as the Sandwich Islands, Twain discovered the white suit that would become his trademark attire later in life. Here he is, dressed in white on a visit to the Catskills.

The speedy propeller- and wind-driven *Ajax* left San Francisco to the blare of a brass band in the middle of a chill March day in 1866. Almost five years before, when Twain had boarded the stagecoach in Missouri, he'd known he'd be traveling west, but not that he'd stroll almost halfway to China.

Emancipated from care and deadlines aboard ship, he lounged about, observing the deckhands at work. "I took a tranquil delight in the kind of labor which is such a luxury . . . —to wit, the labor of other people."

The *Ajax* quickly hit stormy seas, plunging and rolling and sending most of the thirty passengers to the rails with seasickness. For comedy relief, Twain invented a character on the spot for his reports, a blustering traveler named Mr. Brown. Whether or not Twain was among the sufferers, he doesn't say, but phantom Mr. Brown moves among the sick with hearty comfort and loud, irritating advice.

"That's all right—that's all right, you know—it'll clean you out like a jug, and then you won't feel so ornery and smell so ridiculous."

Brown would not be the only specter Twain would take on his travels. A few years later he would pull the same stunt when writing *Roughing It.* Without paying an extra fare, he brought on board the stagecoach a heavily armed but imaginary passenger, George Bemis. It was Bemis who tells the tale of the buffalo that climbed a tree.

His Mississippi River travels aside, Twain had never been on a boiling ocean before and had not developed sea legs. He walked the decks like a drunkard. Nevertheless, he regarded the 2,400-mile voyage as an epic and pleasant adventure.

He planned to spend a month "raking" the islands for impressions to fill his articles, for which he would be paid twenty dollars each. Stand-up comedy had not yet been invented. Newspaper readers were looking to journalists like him for laugh lines.

Docking in balmy Honolulu, the ship was greeted by a Sunday crowd of hundreds, for whom an arrival from the outside world was a celebration. For the first time, Mark saw Sandwich Islanders in bright colors and maidens gaily festooned with necklaces of fresh flowers. And for the first time, this boy from the Midwest would taste mangoes, guavas, and cherimoyas. He tried the fruit of the tamarind tree and it put such a sharp edge on his teeth that "I could have shaved with them."

Everywhere he looked, he recognized fodder for his articles. In Honolulu, "I saw cats—Tom cats, Mary Ann cats, long-tailed cats, bobtailed cats, blind cats, one-eyed cats, walleyed cats, gray cats, black cats, white cats, yellow cats, striped cats, spotted cats, tame cats, wild cats, singed cats, individual cats, groups of cats, platoons of cats, companies of cats, regiments of cats, armies of cats, multitudes of cats, millions of cats, and all of them sleek, fat, lazy, and sound asleep."

Mark Twain's best travel subject was himself. His globe trottings rarely read as if they had been snatched from an encyclopedia. On his first night in Honolulu, he'd made a quick study of the natural history of the island when he sat down and discovered "two million mosquitoes . . . [who] . . . will never sing again."

He rented a horse whose "convulsive" canter reminded him of a San Francisco earthquake, followed by the plunging of the *Ajax* at sea. On his third day in the tropics, he had ridden all day in a saddle that fit him like a shovel, a horseback endurance he was not accustomed to. "I have a delicacy about sitting down," he wrote, evidently sparing further assault on the winged varmints.

And while mosquitoes would be nothing new to his readers, the island was a cabinet of curiosities to open and report upon. He advised travelers to examine the sheets for escaped centipedes before climbing into bed. When it came to scorpions or hairy tarantulas "on stilts," he recommended throwing spittoons at them.

Despite the travails of travel, he fell under the spell of island life. "I breathed in the balmy fragrance of jessamine, oleander, and the Pride of India." Unlike the bare brownstones of San Francisco, here were white cottages with green shutters trimmed with ginger blossoms. In the cool shadows, island girls displayed themselves in floral dresses and lingered free of bustle and care.

He was disappointed to discover that a cabal of scandalized missionaries and white planters had managed to outlaw the celebrated hula dance, at least during daylight hours. Those were hours reserved for laboring in the fields. After a stiff payment of ten dollars to the authorities, the forbidden dance might be performed after work and behind closed doors.

With the performers ticketed for Hell by the missionaries, the island dance was doomed to vanish from sight—or so Twain feared—as a result of foreign interference. He would later write, "Nothing so needs reforming as other people's habits." It was not often that Twain missed the mark, but his bleak prediction has not come to pass. The hula remains as eternal as the trade winds.

He was soon to discover the amazing spectacle of islanders

pressing wooden boards to their chests and riding waves to shore with the speed of tsunamis. Mark sampled this curious sport for himself. He borrowed a primitive surfboard, caught a wave, and took off. "The board struck the shore . . . without any cargo." He was busy underwater, arms and legs boxing the compass.

On another occasion, he came upon native girls bathing in the sea and confessed that he "went and sat down on their clothes to keep them from being stolen."

His letters, with their grace notes of humor, reached Sacramento and were rushed into print. They quickly captured an audience. The San Francisco newspapers reprinted the pieces, and Twain's local celebrity was given an extra polish.

His month of beachcombing and "luxurious vagrancy" stretched into more than four. He began taking notes in an attempt to learn the vowel-heavy language. He began to dream of making a permanent return to the tropics.

He wrote some twenty-five articles of varying lengths. In one of the last ones, he recorded visiting Kealakekua Bay on Kona with his invented sidekick, Mr. Brown.

It was here that Captain Cook had been gracious enough to

The author rode a surfboard—once.

discover the Sandwich Islanders and shoot off a few cannons. The islanders didn't know they had been lost and fired a few spears in response. The great sea captain was killed in an old lava field, roasted, and possibly eaten.

Looking for some sort of memorial, Twain could find only a coconut stump, buttressed by lava rocks and covered over with weathered sheets of ship's copper. The crude inscription, looking as if it had been incised with a nail, identified the spot as the scene of the crime.

Twain and Brown became separated on the remote island, a neat writer's trick. When the newspaperman again sighted the invisible man, Brown was "toiling up the hill in the distance, with a heavy burden on his shoulders. . . . Brown arrived at last, puffing like a steamboat, and gently eased his ponderous burden to the ground—the coconut stump sheathed with copper memorials to the illustrious Captain Cook.

"'Heaven and earth!' I said. 'What are you going to do with that?'

"'Going to do with it!'" replies Twain's satire of the ugly traveler. "'(L)emme blow a little—it's monstrous heavy, that log is. . . . Why, I'm going to take her home for a specimen.'

"'You egregious ass! March straight back again and put it where you got it.'"

When Twain sailed out of Honolulu on a return voyage to San Francisco, he left the "shameless" Mr. Brown marooned and forgotten under a palm tree.

CHAPTER TWENTY

THE TROUBLE BEGINS AT 8

AID TWAIN, "I RETURNED TO CALIFORNIA TO FIND myself about the best-known honest man on the Pacific Coast."

He checked back into the Occidental Hotel, but it had lost its charms for him. With fresh memories of the flower-scented tropics, he felt grumpy to be in a bricks-and-mortar city. He saw life around him moving with the clatter of runaway horses. He missed the island pace and its balmy breezes. It was August, and he would write a line still locally quoted as proof of residency. "The coldest winter I ever spent was a summer day in San Francisco."

Not enthusiastic about returning to the drudgery of daily news-papering, he began revising his Sandwich Island pieces with a hope of emerging in a new career as a book author. He was too savvy to expect fame to keep energizing itself like a perpetual motion machine. He'd have to continually nourish it.

Other authors had launched their literary works as young men. Dickens had published *Oliver Twist* at age twenty-five. Melville had been hardly older than Twain himself when he wrote the massive adventure *Moby-Dick*. What had Twain to show for his ambitions? A literary trinket about a jumping frog.

He would be getting a late start, and rushed to revise his Sandwich Island idyll.

He sent it east, where publishers insulted him by rejecting it.

Despite the jingle of coins remaining in his pockets, the future now looked uncertain and depressing. His ironclad optimism quickly rusted out. He later confessed to holding a gun to his head, but that seemed to have had less conviction in it than stage business and dramatic flare. Exaggeration in life and in his fiction was the oxygen of his genius.

Enter Thomas Maguire. He had a scheme to make Twain rich at last. A theater owner, Maguire urged Mark to "strike while the iron was hot—break into the lecture field!"

In Virginia City, Twain had heard his friend, the humorist

Artemus Ward, on the lecture platform. Ward, who delivered comedy sketches as a Yankee showman bucksawing the English language into illiterate sawdust, had filled the small opera house with laughter.

Could Twain do that? Mark wasn't sure. He had little experience at public speaking. And San Francisco had shown little enthusiasm for lectures as entertainment and enlightenment. He hesitated.

But friends persuaded him to give it a whirl. Maguire offered his new and huge opera houses on Pine Street for one night at half price, fifty dollars—payable from the ticket receipts. Another friend slapped him on the back.

"And charge a dollar a ticket!"

The lofty admission price dumbfounded Twain. A dollar could buy a seven-course dinner at a restaurant, with change left over for the tip. But he did not have a gift for caution. If he could fill the theater at that ticket price, he'd be rich. How many friends in possession of a dollar did he have? How many seats did the opera house hold? Fifteen hundred? Two thousand?

He went at the preparations with his coattails on fire. He wrote out his hour-plus lecture, and then composed advertising lines that would be stolen widely by less talented promoters across the country. Instead of promising that the curtain would rise at eight in the evening, Mark wrote: "The Trouble to begin at 8 o'clock."

He spent $150 of his dwindling fortune on publicity to paper the town and to warn the innocents. And to stir up a few laughs in advance.

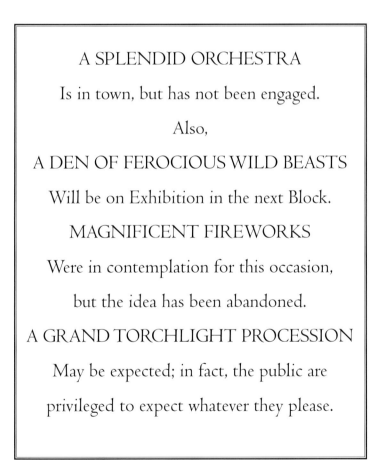

A SPLENDID ORCHESTRA

Is in town, but has not been engaged.

Also,

A DEN OF FEROCIOUS WILD BEASTS

Will be on Exhibition in the next Block.

MAGNIFICENT FIREWORKS

Were in contemplation for this occasion,

but the idea has been abandoned.

A GRAND TORCHLIGHT PROCESSION

May be expected; in fact, the public are

privileged to expect whatever they please.

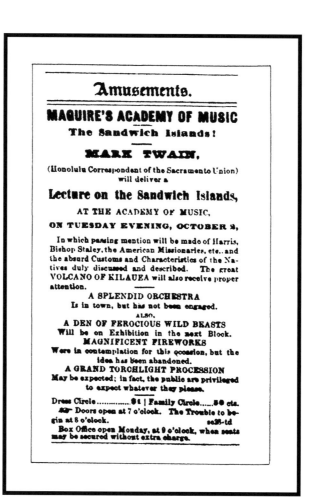

In 1866, on the night of October 2, the author backed into a new career as a public lecturer. Here, in his first advertisement, he promised a phantom orchestra and, lower right, "The Trouble to begin at 8 o'clock."

And then stage fright set in. He could eat nothing the day of his coming disaster. He was certain that his tongue would freeze up and that his knees would sound like rattlesnakes. He thought of fleeing town to cure his acute misery. On the other hand, what if no one showed up to see him? That possibility was more terrifying than stage fright.

Early in October, on the appointed night, he dragged himself to the empty theater. Before long, to his mixed horror and pleasure, the house began filling up. Soon there was standing room only. It appeared that the San Francisco elite had turned up in starched shirts and evening dress, and was now waiting for the trouble to begin.

Finally, the audience commenced stamping its feet to bring the performer on. Even the governor was out there hammering the floor.

Mark Twain, at stage left, could wait no longer. Like a moth drawn to a perilous flame, he found himself shambling into the footlights. "The tumult in my heart and brain and legs continued a full minute before I could gain any command over myself. . . . little by little my fright melted away, and I began to talk. Within three or four minutes, I was comfortable, and even content."

He opened with an apology, speaking in his unhurried Missouri drawl. Explaining that the orchestra had backed out, he said that he had managed to engage a trombonist.

But when the musician discovered the circumstances, he too backed out, protesting that unlike Twain, "he wasn't going to make a fool of himself by sitting on the stage and blowing his horn all by himself."

That role was now left to Twain. On the pretext of a lecture on the Sandwich Islands, he served up his first laughs.

"The natives are a very hospitable people indeed—very hospitable. . . . They will feed you on baked dog, or poi, or raw fish, or raw salt pork, or fricasseed cat—all the luxuries of the season."

He continued, "They are fond of dogs . . . a species of little mean cur. . . . there is nothing attractive about these dogs. . . . unless it is their bushy tails. A friend of mine said if he had one of those dogs he would cut off the tail and throw the rest of the dog away."

The charge of cannibalism on the island was a slander, remarked Twain. "They didn't eat Captain Cook—or if they did it was only for fun. . . . In other cities, I usually illustrate cannibalism, but I am a

Mark Twain on the lecture platform. He was a bemusing target for cartoonists.

stranger here, and don't feel like taking liberties. Still, if anyone in the audience will loan me an infant I will illustrate the matter."

With laughter safely airborne, his trombone solo was quickly bouncing off the opera house ceiling. He got a standing ovation.

THE TROUBLE IS OVER, headlined a review the next day. "The inimitable Mark Twain . . ."

He was a hit. He was a sensation.

Like a man shot out of a cannon, he had launched himself on a new career. It would pay the rent. Literature would have to cool its heels.

CHAPTER TWENTY-ONE

THE GREAT HOLDUP

TWAIN MADE PLANS TO REPEAT HIS LECTURE IN Sacramento and in the California mining camps sporting opera houses—such cultural boomtowns as Red Dog, Gouge Eye, or You Bet. And then he'd return to Nevada and Virginia City to strut upon the stage of Piper's Opera House.

Meanwhile, he tinkered with his program, adding comic riffs as pertinent to the Sandwich Islands as square dancing.

Everyone in the West knew the stagecoach tale about Horace Greeley, the famous New York newspaper publisher, and his stage driver, Hank Monk. Twain couldn't resist confounding his audience by telling the familiar story—in his own way.

It was Greeley who had coined the phrase "Go west, young

man." Taking his own advice, he had gone west and was late for an engagement in Placerville, California. He urged thundering haste upon his stagecoach driver.

"Keep your seat, Horace, I'll get you there on time!"

The coach took off in a cloud of dust. Greeley kept leaning forward, demanding even more horsepower.

"Keep your seat, Horace, I'll get you there on time!"

Hank Monk cracked his whip . . . the coach bounced up and down in such a way that it jolted the buttons all off of Horace's coat and finally shot his head clean through the roof of the stage.

"Keep your seat, Horace, I'll get you there on time," Monk shouted.

Twain, puffing a cigar, managed to extract unexpected laughs out of the tale. "Keep your seat, Horace," was quoted in the hills as if it were a sacred line from Homer. What Horace Greeley had to do with the Sandwich Islands was a mystery; it would not be the first time the lecturer seemed to wander from his subject to track down a laugh. It was part of his stage charm and seduction.

He was welcomed to Nevada like a prodigal son. Virginia City stuffed Piper's Opera House with old friends, including bantam Steve Gillis, still at the *Enterprise*.

A week later, on a freezing November night, Twain and his tour manager were returning on foot from a lecture in nearby Gold Hill when he felt someone thrust "a horrible six-shooter in my face," and shout, "Stand and deliver!"

Six masked desperadoes had pounced upon them with the lights of Virginia City not far off. Twain remained cool. To the demand that he deliver his valuables, he replied, "My son, your arguments are powerful—take what I have, but unlock that powerful pistol."

"No remarks! Put up your hands. Hand over your money!"

Mark lifted his hands above his head. "Certainly—"

"Are you going to hand out your money or *not*! By george, you want the head shot off you awful bad!"

"Well, friend . . . you tell me to give up my money, and when I reach for it you tell me to put up my hands."

The ruffians lifted Twain's watch and a carpetbag half-filled with silver from the night's lecture. Posting a couple of gunmen behind the boulders, the remaining outlaws faded back along the road to Virginia City. They left a grim warning for the two victims to remain standing with their arms in the air for ten minutes. Move, and Mark would be shot.

A moment of high drama in Twain's lectures came when he described Horace Greeley's famous stagecoach ride.

In the far-off East, the artist's befuddled rendering of the great holdup hoax. He overlooked black masks for the desperadoes, for Twain would have recognized them as Steve Gillis and other friends with silver dollars in their mouths to disguise their voices.

A prestigious residential street in Virginia City. It was on an approach to town like this that Twain suffered the humiliation of being held up.

Teeth chattering with the cold, Twain decided to stand an extra five minutes, presumably in the event the desperadoes were consulting his watch, which might be running fast.

Finally the two victims tramped into a saloon on C Street, where they ran into newspaper friends. Mark explained that they had been robbed. Twain was as "unruffled as a mountain lake," recalled Steve Gillis, who happened to be there. Twain borrowed a hundred dollars from his old sidekick in order to call for a round of drinks. Unknown to him, it was his own silver, recently taken at gunpoint, that Steve handed him.

The robbery had been a hoax. It had been a practical joke, devised by the mischievous Gillis himself. Mark's friends had worn black masks and slipped silver dollars into their mouths to alter their voices. But one of the *Enterprise*'s journalists had not been apprised of the hoax and had filed the story of Twain's humiliation at the hands of masked bandits. It made news as far off as New York.

If Mark had been calm during the robbery, he was now "mad clear through," Gillis recalled.

Years later, the celebrated author left the humiliating hoax out of his autobiography.

Chapter Twenty-Two
TWAIN ATTEMPTS TO BEHAVE

WHEN MARK TWAIN RETURNED TO SAN FRANCISCO, he stepped off the Overland stagecoach a changed man. He was peacock rich. He had developed a charismatic stage persona that would last a lifetime: It was rustic Sam Clemens in French cuffs. His Missouri drawl was polished. He maintained an innocent expression when launching his earnest whoppers, followed by the baffled pause and a lift of an eyebrow when one of his remarks produced laughter.

Most affecting, he'd heard applause. In the past his quips had gone out into the silent world of print. Like many young journalists, he'd learned to write them to fill space at the ragged ends of stories. For the first time he was hearing thunderclaps of merriment and approval.

His descriptive and entertaining powers had not escaped the eye of the *Daily Alta California*, a hard-nosed San Francisco newspaper. When Twain proposed that he take a trip around the world at the expense of the paper, the proprietors agreed. In exchange, the journalist would write a series of articles, much like the ones he had posted from the Sandwich Islands.

But Twain stumbled across richer fodder for his talents in a pricey five-month pleasure cruise to the Mediterranean, ending with a pilgrimage to the Holy Land. It was being organized by wealthy Protestants who had persuaded the Civil War hero General William Tecumseh Sherman, among other prominent Christians, to sign up for the uplifting voyage.

By this stage of his life, Twain had shed religious convictions like bark off a tree, but he remained tolerant toward others not similarly in rebellion. From time to time he would drop in on a Presbyterian service, the church of his childhood, to check the goings-on.

Good intentions aside, he was bound to be a weed among the daffodils. A San Francisco clergyman had already searched out Sam's family tree and determined him to be "This son of the devil, Mark Twain."

Discovering himself to be free of horns and a tail, Twain slipped out of San Francisco for New York to await the ark leased for the pilgrimage, the paddlewheel steamboat *Quaker City*.

Finding ample time to spare, he gave his Sandwich Island lecture before a crowd of three thousand in Brooklyn. Since this was not the rowdy West, but the effete East, he altered his poster line to read, "The Wisdom will begin to flow at 8." Delivering wisdom or trouble, he was a hit.

The weather was stormy when Twain boarded the *Quaker City* for the voyage across the Atlantic. Despite the sanctified nature of its passenger list, the seas outside the harbor were rough and wildly baptismal. The vessel took shelter and dropped anchor. The pilgrimage was delayed. With its two bulky sidewheels, the ship appeared to be wearing wooden earmuffs against the cold winds.

Once the weather brightened and the ship got under way, Twain discovered that smoking, swearing, and card playing would be frowned upon. And that there would be prayer meetings every night. Perhaps he'd been wrong; perhaps there was a Hell, after all, and he'd bought a first-class ticket.

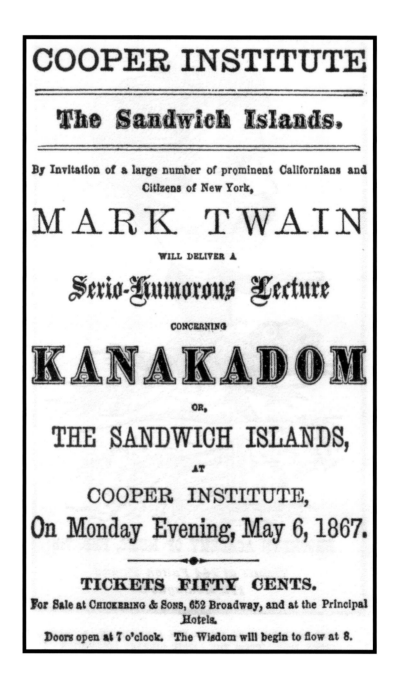

COOPER INSTITUTE

The Sandwich Islands.

By Invitation of a large number of prominent Californians and Citizens of New York,

MARK TWAIN

WILL DELIVER A

Serio-Humorous Lecture

CONCERNING

KANAKADOM

OR,

THE SANDWICH ISLANDS,

AT

COOPER INSTITUTE,

On Monday Evening, May 6, 1867.

TICKETS FIFTY CENTS.

For Sale at CHICKERING & SONS, 652 Broadway, and at the Principal Hotels.

Doors open at 7 o'clock. The Wisdom will begin to flow at 8.

Assuming that he would be speaking to a more sophisticated audience in well-bred New York, he changed the notice to "The Wisdom will begin to flow at 8." Kanaka was an early term for Hawaiian Islanders.

He tried to avoid stepping on any pious toes. Hoping to conduct himself as a gentleman, he volunteered to sing with the choir. He would behave himself. But his goodwill and restraint would be put to extreme tensions.

So straight and narrow were his fellow passengers that the captain was asked to stop his ship on Sunday in midocean to respect the Sabbath.

Earlier, General Sherman had canceled out, and Twain was pleased to be moved up to the general's luxurious Cabin Ten. In due time, it became the center of mutiny when a few less pious passengers, calling themselves the Nighthawks, gathered to play cards and light expensive cigars. Twain had had the foresight to bring his preferred rustic brand.

When he reached Europe to render the old cities and their artifacts into words, he largely restrained his impulse toward burlesque. He was moved to awe by the vast grandeur of Versailles, with a staff of 36,000 laborers to maintain it. His awe was undiminished when he laid eyes on the women of Genoa, Italy, whom he declared to be the most beautiful in the world.

But he couldn't bring himself to feel humbled daily and hourly by the Old Country's arrogant treasures. Some of the ancient marble statuary he felt to be inferior to wooden Indians at cigar stores at home. He gazed at Mount Vesuvius and described it as a mere soup kettle compared with a volcano he'd seen in the Sandwich Islands.

He was not moved to tears when shown a nail from the True Cross. He'd already seen enough of them in old churches "to fill a nail keg."

He chose to play the part of the ugly American long before the role had been invented. But he did it with charm and whimsy. It was not difficult to detect something in his cheek—his tongue.

In the Holy Land he contemplated the miracle of Moses needing forty years to cross the desert. The Overland stage, he said, could have done it in thirty-six hours. When a boatman at the Sea of Galilee overcharged him, he remarked, "Do you wonder now that Christ walked?"

As the months of travel wore on, Twain's patience with his fellow passengers wore thin. His moods gave way to snorts and mutterings. He was discovering the wealthy pilgrims to be mean, gullible, sanctimonious, penny-pinching, and vandals of souvenirs.

On their excursion to the Holy Land, modern pilgrims on the *Quaker City* held nightly church services despite bilious seasickness. They asked the captain to stop the ship on the Sabbath.

THE RELIC-HUNTER.

Twain was appalled to see his fellow travelers chipping away at the Sphinx for souvenirs.

An illustration in *The Innocents Abroad* shows a passenger on a tall ladder chipping away at the Sphinx.

When he debarked in New York, his contempt for the low breeding of mankind was fixed in marble. As a parting shot, he declared the voyage to have been "a funeral excursion without a corpse."

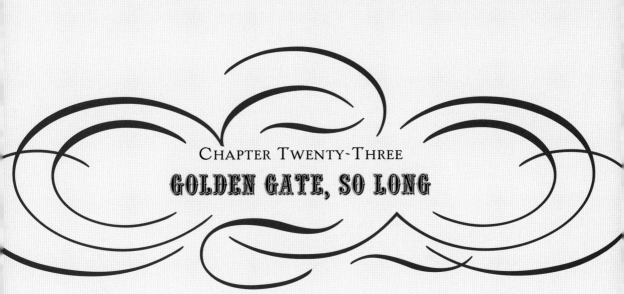

CHAPTER TWENTY-THREE
GOLDEN GATE, SO LONG

WHEN TWAIN RETURNED TO HIS NEST AT THE Occidental Hotel in San Francisco, it was to prepare his travel notes for a book. But the *Alta California* had light-fingered the publishing rights.

As he had dispatched his original articles, and as they had been printed week by week, the newspaper had copyrighted the series in its own name. In a legal sense, the newspaper had become the author of Mark Twain's distinctive prose. It owned the words.

Twain flew into a fury and invaded the newspaper office like a Missouri tornado full of grit and spare parts. In the end, he came out holding the book rights in his fist.

From the earlier, hastily composed tales, he rewrote *The Innocents*

Twain's hair turned white to match his suits, but his red mustache was hanging on to his youth in the West.

I am writing from the grave.

A sample of Mark Twain's handwriting. He was always looking ahead.

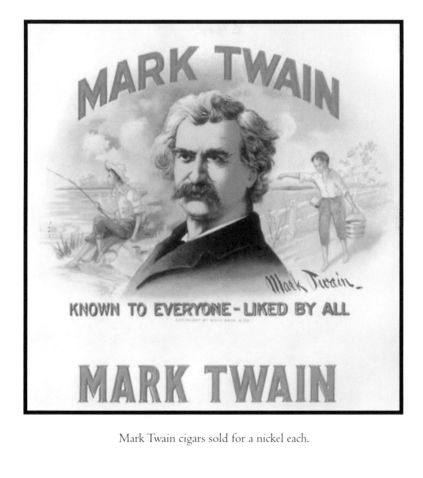

Mark Twain cigars sold for a nickel each.

Abroad, as his adventure would be called, squeezing out "some of the wind and water." Writing eleven and twelve hours a day, "I did 200,000 words in sixty days." This by a man once regarded by his best newspaper friend, Steve Gillis, as lazy.

The book was published in August 1869. It became one of the great bestsellers of the century, still in print almost 150 years later.

At last! Mark Twain had succeeded in achieving the glory and fortune that had driven him ever since his village beginnings as the real-life Tom Sawyer.

At age thirty-three, his literary apprenticeship had come to an end. He had stored enough experience and raw material to last him a lifetime. Except for his Missouri drawl, he had changed beyond recognition into a man of the world. His wit had spent years at the grinding stone and was now as sharp and deadly as a cornered porcupine.

He packed his bags and left San Francisco, not to return for thirty years. He would begin a new life in the East. Novels, short stories, essays, and travel books followed. His literary revels in the Wild West had shifted scenery and furniture. He now did his writing in the billiard room of his own house, or in the comfort of his own bed. His name went up in lights even before Edison invented the lightbulb.

He dined in the White House with Theodore Roosevelt. He became a confidant of General Ulysses S. Grant. He lived in England and Italy and tangled with the German language, abandoning it with dueling scars. His whimsies kept flowing. When a rumor surfaced that he had died, he responded with one of his most frequently cited snorts. "The report of my death is greatly exaggerated." Hotels were named after him. Steamboats were named after him. A brand of five-cent cigars was named after him, an honor normally reserved for kings, princes, and Spanish dancers. He made a leisurely trip around the world, but took notes. An admirer sent him a letter addressed, "Mark Twain, God Knows Where."

Many weeks passed before Twain answered from Italy. "He did."

CHAPTER TWENTY-FOUR
AFTERSTORY

 HAT HAPPENED NEXT?

Mark Twain fell in love. He called her Livy. She was Olivia Louise Langdon, daughter of a wealthy coal man from Elmira, New York. Blue-eyed, with brown hair parted down the center, she was delicate but lovely, better educated than Mark, and privileged. They married in February 1870. With the surprise gift of a house from the bride's father, complete with silverware and servants, Mark took up residence in Buffalo, New York.

He resumed lecturing, this time on the Holy Land trip, sometimes under the peevish title "The Vandals Abroad." The *Quaker City* went on to become a Cuban gunrunner. As if in a fit of chagrin, it blew a boiler and sank near Bermuda.

Mark Twain's wife, Olivia Clemens.

Soon his old San Francisco friend Bret Harte briefly eclipsed Twain's own fame with the publication of *Outcasts of Poker Flat* and *The Luck of Roaring Camp*. Along the stops traveling to the east, Harte created the sensation of a rock star today. He became the American ambassador to England and vanished from Twain's life, owing Mark thousands of dollars.

Meanwhile, Twain was at work whimsically recalling the stagecoach trip to the Wild West that he and his brother Orion had taken nine years before. *Roughing It* remains perhaps the most physical and adventurous of his travel books, which include *The Innocents Abroad* and *Following the Equator*.

Livy was busy with motherhood. A son, Langdon, was born, followed by daughters Susy, Clara, and Jean. Twain built a larger house in Hartford, Connecticut.

Soon he would learn to ride a bicycle and attempt his first novel, *The Gilded Age*. As Twain had been sneaking fiction into his nonfiction for a decade, the demands of a novel to create believable characters would have been well-practiced sleight-of-hand to him.

A sprawling satire on American life and the flash and lure of easy riches, *The Gilded Age* was written in collaboration with a journalist and neighbor, Charles Dudley Warner. It was here that first appeared the quip that refuses to roll over and die. "Everyone complains about the weather, but no one does anything about it." Neither author saw air conditioning over the horizon.

These literary works were finger exercises for the novel on its way, *The Adventures of Tom Sawyer*. In the summer of 1874, Twain sat down to cast in literary bronze his boyhood in Hannibal, Missouri. Tom Sawyer was born—curly haired and about nine years old.

Tom has a natural gift for misbehavior and cunning. He's a show-off. He plays hooky. He plays pirate. He witnesses a murder in a graveyard. He seeks buried treasure. And he has a crush on his school friend Becky Thatcher. Together, they get lost in a dark and sinister cave for three days. Movies are made about him.

The novel has never dropped out of sight since the day it was first published in 1876. Tom and his runaway friend, Huckleberry Finn, became the most famous boys in American literature.

The reader of Huckleberry's own novel is met with a warning when turning the title page. Wrote Twain:

NOTICE

Persons attempting to find a motive in this narrative will be prosecuted; persons attempting to find a moral in it will be banished; persons attempting to find a plot in it will be shot.

Adventures of Huckleberry Finn is written in Huck's own voice and with his own best barefoot grammar. "The Widow Douglas," he writes, "she took me for her son, and allowed she would sivilize me. . . . when I couldn't stand it no longer, I lit out."

Soon he flees a drunken and abusing father and hides on an island in the river. Like Robinson Crusoe, he discovers signs that someone else is hiding there. The stranger turns out to be Jim, a runaway slave.

Continuing their escape, the two float down the river on a raft in one of the great voyages in literature. Despite gross differences of birth, they watch out for each other. Scenes range from the humorous and comic to the fearful and gripping. Huck disguises himself and sneaks into town. He learns that folks believe he has been murdered and that the runaway slave, Jim, is being hunted as the murderer.

The runaways continue their rafting saga. Despite Twain's notice, there is a plot. Like the Mississippi River, the plot jumps its banks from time to time, forming islands, horseshoe bends, and detours. But the power of the tide is so strong that it carries Mark Twain's outraged conscience along under full flood. At the end, Huck writes, "If I'd a knowed what a trouble it was to make a book I wouldn't a tackled it."

The trouble was that Twain's novels were oral storytelling writ large. This permitted him to ramble about without a compass and occasionally to get lost in byways and burlesques. How could he resist the rats and snakes late in chapter 39, even though they barely advance the plot toward its conclusion? And why did he bring Tom Sawyer back on stage toward the end of Huck's book if it wasn't to help the bewildered author find a way out of the confounded novel?

While *Tom Sawyer* had taken only a year to write, Twain struggled with *Huckleberry Finn* over a period of seven years. He shelved it twice for long periods of time and in frustration threatened to burn the manuscript.

Twain had no idea that he was writing a masterpiece. He declared

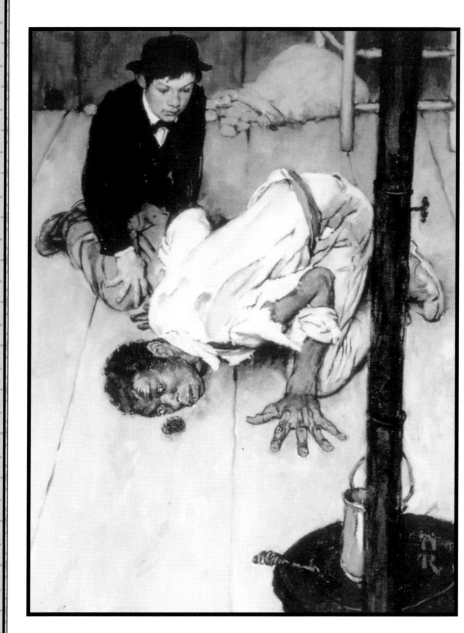

Twain's scorn for superstitious nonsense was a recipe for humor in Huckleberry Finn, when Jim strains to listen for a spirit's voice in a hairball from an ox's stomach. The enchanted tangle predicts that Huck will be hung. The hairy spirit was confused.

Alone on the raft, Jim believes that young Huck has drowned during a heavy fog. Twain quickly turns the tenderness of the moment into burlesque when Huck attempts to trick the slave into believing the death was a dream. Jim won't be fooled and is resentful of Huck's boyish cruelty.

he liked the novel "tolerably well," valuing it less than others of his books.

That he got lost in the plot for long periods of time reveals that he improvised his stories as he went along. Working without detailed outlines in advance is a surprisingly common practice among novelists. *Pinocchio,* among other famous stories, was a similar improvisation.

As a newspaperman, Twain knew how to marshal facts and spin them out amusingly on paper. That's why he was able to write up his Holy Land travels at three thousand words a day. At that rate, he should have been able to write *Tom Sawyer,* a mere seventy thousand words, in less than a month. Plot could be bewitching to read, but bewildering to create and manage. Twain had to learn to do it on the job.

Gloom and depression were uninvited guests to Twain's celebrations of public approval and adoration. As the years wore on, funereal moods became a close companion. He had lost his two-year-old son to diphtheria. His daughter Susy would be struck by spinal meningitis. Jean, his youngest child, would have an epileptic seizure in the bathtub and die. Livy was not well. Twain's fate was crushing him.

Except for Clara, he would see his entire family die before him.

His bleak view of life became as frozen and fixed as the north star. His last novel, written in 1892, *Pudd'nhead Wilson*, was his most troubled. While it takes the rough form of a detective story, and was the first to use the new tool of fingerprinting, it deals with the social cruelty of slave days in a Mississippi town much like Hannibal. One look-alike boy is accepted by society as white, the other rejected as black, but they were switched as infants. It's *The Prince and the Pauper* draped in black.

Bitterness aside, Twain was never able to abandon his gift for laughter. All he had to do was look around. The unshod boy from Hannibal now had a butler.

He wasn't convinced that he had a natural gift for the novel, but his bookshelf contradicts him. *A Connecticut Yankee in King Arthur's Court*, for example, is among the most successful time-travel stories ever written. An American inventor suffers a blow to the head and awakens in sixth-century England, and the fun begins.

Mark Twain's hard-earned fortune soon collapsed. Like his father investing in a perpetual motion machine, he invested in a new-fangled and complicated contraption that would set type for printing. It was a wonderful idea to eliminate the tedium of hand-setting letters made of lead, but this machine didn't work properly. Later, similar inventions by others would succeed.

When additional investments turned sour as well, Twain went bankrupt. He was under no legal obligation to pay off his debts, but to Twain it was a point of honor to do so.

While he claimed to loathe lecturing, it was the only way he knew to recoup his losses. He set off on a breathless tour, speaking in twenty-two cities in a month. He kept talking, tramping from platform to opera house with ever-changing footlights.

As his hair turned white, so did his wardrobe. His snowy suits now marked him as instantly as the Eiffel Tower identified Paris. At the same time, he tossed off trade secrets that have become immortal and sacred to the generations of writers who followed.

"The difference between the right word and the almost right word is the difference between lightning and the lightning bug."

In a war with unnecessary adjectives, he said, "When in doubt, strike it out."

From his writing study, Mark Twain might be gazing back on his ramble-scramble life, from Missouri ragamuffin to New England country squire. He now wore French cuffs on his shirts, but retained his dazzling skill in exercising the village art and glory of cussing.

And "A successful book is not made of what is in it, but what is left out of it."

A friend he never lost touch with was his old editor at the Virginia City *Territorial Enterprise*. Joe Goodman had sold the paper and tried growing grapes in Central California. After making and losing a fortune, he devoted twelve years of his life to writing a scholarly book on Maya hieroglyphics.

As for mischief-making Steve Gillis, who had nudged Clemens into a duel, the fearless newspaperman spent most of his life on the *Enterprise*. He outlived Mark Twain by several years.

Twain's older brother, Orion, pursued failed ambitions to the end of his life, in 1897. He even schemed of getting rich with the notion of a flying machine. For once, he was right, but the new enterprise collapsed. Mark had largely supported him throughout his later life.

The author was now so celebrated that his portrait looked out from postage stamps and was shuffled among the cards in the pack for the game of Authors. He was so quotable that a critic styled him "the American Shakespeare, only funnier."

He outlived his wife, Livy, by six tormented years. Right up until the end, he stormed about injustice, "money-lust," bigotry, and the general foolishness of man, himself included. In a letter he confessed, "I have been an author for twenty years, and an ass for fifty-five."

The fuse on his temper grew shorter through the years. He was apt to explode and disturb the household over a button missing from his shirt. Writing to his friend the author and editor William Dean Howells, he expressed shock and pain to discover in 1897 that his beloved daughters had been afraid of him.

How had such a charming and joyous young man turned into a charming but bitter tyrant and spitfire, cussing out humanity? It would have been a mystery had he *not* changed. He was the author and critic with piercing X-ray eyes. He saw with disappointed vision the treacheries and public deceptions that went largely ignored. It was not the poor who were inheriting the earth, he saw; it was the greedy, the pretenders, and the ruthless.

And there was the constant bastinado, a form of slow torture by striking the soles of the foot, described in *Innocents Abroad*, that beset his family. In his Hannibal childhood, he had watched a younger brother and sister die, followed not long after by another brother. Now, as a father, he watched an infant son and two daughters vanish. Grief had designated him an eternal pallbearer.

With a dramatist's sense of timing, he famously died of heart disease on April 21 in 1910—the year that Halley's comet was due to return. The cosmic body was meticulous in keeping its date with the cosmic Mark Twain.

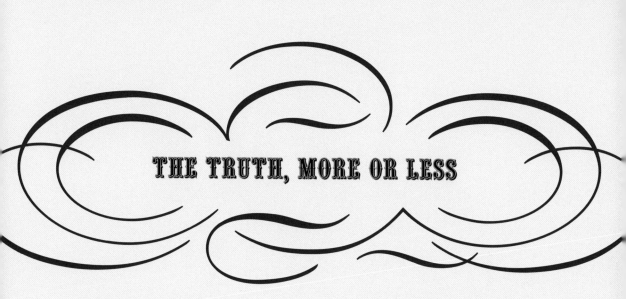

THE TRUTH, MORE OR LESS

THE BIOGRAPHER'S FIRST OBLIGATION IS TO SMOKE out fictions and overblown exaggerations in rendering a celebrated life. What is one to do with Mark Twain, who believed, "A lie well told is immortal"?

He was, by instinct and long practice, a storyteller. Scribbling away at the events of his autobiography, he can be seen moving the furniture around from time to time to highlight or sharpen the story. He once confessed that he remembered things whether they happened or not. He claimed that he had given up lying, for it was overrun with amateurs. That was a whimsical lie.

Did he really show up for the duel way back in chapter 13? A small body of opinion has surfaced that flatly regards the story as fanciful.

The details so perfectly mesh that one might easily suspect we are seeing Twain's literary carpentry at work. The story may be embraced as gospel if only on the unchallenged fact that he and Steve Gillis, who confirmed the story, had to flee town on the next stagecoach. Embellishments in the tale aside, I'm inclined to throw in with Twain and Gillis.

You'll recall that Twain invented two travel companions: Bemis in *Roughing It*, and Mr. Brown in the Hawaiian adventure. Today, such shell games played in books of nonfiction would be sure to inspire newspaper scandals. But deception was never one of Twain's pastimes. One needs to credit the author with exalted standards as a reporter, while allowing for a sly literary wink now and then. He created these roguish characters as entertainment, as travel jesters. They were, in short, ventriloquist's dummies, with Twain himself working the levers. They provided alternate comic voices.

Twain and the fortune-tellers. Some commentators credit Mark with a sincere embrace of fortune-telling, phrenology, and other intoxications. I doubt it. He blew wise to the technique of "cold reading": tricking the subject into betraying personal details by unguarded speech and, as already mentioned, spotting clues from details of clothing and demeanor.

This is the stock-in-trade of charlatans. Here, fortune-tellers anticipated Sherlock Holmes, who could determine a stranger's London neighborhood by the color of a mud daub on his shoe. Later Twain made it a point to visit the clairvoyants incognito. His thundering doubts on the subject were deafening.

He had no hesitation, on the other hand, in making alterations to humble facts for the swordplay of his wit. *En garde!* A brilliant example of comic irony is displayed in these widely quoted lines: "When I was a boy of fourteen, my father was so ignorant, I could hardly stand to have the old man around. But when I got to be twenty-one, I was astonished at how much he had learned in seven years."

Who cares that when Twain was fourteen, his father was dead and buried? The observation is true.

And Twain hadn't apprenticed himself at fourteen to Joseph P. Ament and his newspaper shop. The young publisher was yet to take over the *Hannibal Courier* for another year and a half. But condensing time for effect was a writer's stock-in-trade, going back to the early Greek playwrights.

You may recall the account in chapter 17 of Twain and his

partner walking away from pay dirt in a rainstorm, only to return and find a pair of Austrians then in possession of the hole in the ground. Steve Gillis was the source of the story, but even Albert Bigelow Paine had his doubts. Twain omitted the story in his auto-biography. Says a lot.

One hears that Twain lifted his pen name from an ancient mariner of New Orleans, then presumed dead, a scribbling Captain Sellers. Mark says so himself in his autobiography. But impertinent scholars cannot find any truth in it. No earlier Mark Twain bylines can be turned up in New Orleans journals of the period. And Sellers wasn't dead at all.

A hoax would have had no point. It's possible that someone told Sam, in error, that Sellers had already used the river pseudonym. Without bothering to check, Twain would have had the courtesy to give the Mississippi scribbler a grateful salute in passing.

After all, the name then had no cash value.

Nevertheless, one hears the charge of literary theft from many who know little else of Mark Twain. As he himself wrote, "A lie can travel halfway around the world while the truth is putting on its shoes."

WHEN MARK TWAIN PUBLISHED THIS STORY IN book form, he dedicated it to John Smith. He didn't know any of the multitude of John Smiths at large. His playful theory was that anyone to whom a book is dedicated would go out and buy a copy.

Twain tells the frog story in a letter to his old Virginia City friend Artemus Ward. Introducing a narrator, Simon Wheeler, Twain describes the man as fat, bald, and garrulous—a spitting image of Ben Coon, the teller of the tale back in Angel's Camp. We pick up the beginning of the comedy when Twain asks Wheeler about a certain Reverend Leonidas.

The Jumping Frog

DAN'L

"Rev. Leonidas W. H'm, Reverend Le—well, there was a feller here once by the name of *Jim* Smiley, in the winter of '49—or may be it was the spring of '50—I don't recollect exactly, somehow, though what makes me think it was one or the other is because I remember the big flume warn't finished when he first came to the camp; but any way, he was the curiosest man about always betting on anything that turned up you ever see, if he could get anybody to bet on the other side; and if he couldn't he'd change sides. Any way that suited the other man would suit *him*— any way just so's he got a bet, *he* was satisfied. But still he was lucky, uncommon lucky; he most always come out winner. He was always ready and laying for a chance; there couldn't be no solit'ry thing mentioned but that feller'd offer to bet on it, and take any side you please, as I was just telling you. If there was a horse-race, you'd find him flush or you'd find him busted at the end of it; if there was a dog-fight, he'd bet on it; if there was a cat-fight, he'd bet on it; if there was a chicken-fight, he'd bet on it; why, if there was two birds setting on a fence, he would bet you which one would fly first; or if there was a camp-meeting, he would be there reg'lar to bet on Parson Walker, which he judged to be the best exhorter about here, and so he was too, and a good man. If he even see a straddle-bug start to go anywheres, he would bet you how long it would take him to get to—to wherever he was going to, and if you took him up, he would foller that straddle-bug to Mexico but what he would find out where he was bound for and how long he was on the road. Lots of the boys here has seen that Smiley and can tell you about him. Why, it never made no difference to *him*—he'd bet on *any* thing—the dangest feller. Parson Walker's wife laid very sick once, for a good while, and it seemed as if they warn't going to save her; but one morning he come in, and Smiley up and asked him how she was, and he said she was considable better—thank the Lord for his inf'nit mercy—and coming on so smart that with the blessing of Prov'dence she'd get well yet; and Smiley, before he thought, says, "Well, I'll risk two-and-a-half she don't anyway."

Thish-yer Smiley had a mare—the boys called her the fifteen-minute nag, but that was only in fun, you know, because of course she was faster than that—and he used to win money on that horse, for all she was so slow and always had the asthma, or the distemper, or the consumption, or something of that kind. They used to give her two or three hundred yards start, and then pass her under way; but always at the fag-end of the race she'd get excited and desperate-like, and come cavorting and straddling up, and scattering her legs around limber, sometimes in the air, and sometimes out to one side amongst the fences, and kicking up m-o-r-e dust and raising m-o-r-e racket with her coughing and sneezing and blowing her nose—and *always* fetch up at the stand just about a neck ahead, as near as you could cipher it down.

And he had a little small bull-pup, that to look at him you'd think he warn't worth a cent but to set around and look ornery and lay for a chance to steal something. But as soon as money was up on him he was a different dog; his under-jaw'd begin to stick out like the fo'-castle of a steamboat, and his teeth would uncover and shine like the furnaces. And a dog might tackle him and bully-rag him, and bite him, and throw him over his shoulder two or three times, and Andrew Jackson—which was the name of the pup— Andrew Jackson would never let on but what *he* was satisfied, and hadn't expected nothing else—and the bets being doubled and doubled on the other side all the time, till the money was all up; and then all of a sudden he would grab the other dog jest by the j'int of his hind leg and freeze to it—not chaw, you understand, but only just grip and hang on till they throwed up the sponge, if it was a year. Smiley always come out winner on that pup, till he harnessed a dog once that didn't have no hind legs, because they'd been sawed off in a circular saw, and when the thing had gone along far enough, and the money was all up, and he come to make a snatch for his pet holt, he see in a minute how he'd been imposed on, and how the other dog had him in the door, so to speak, and he 'peared surprised, and then he looked sorter discouraged-like, and didn't try no more to win the fight, and so he got shucked out bad. He gave Smiley a look, as much as to say his heart was broke, and it was *his* fault, for putting up a dog that hadn't no hind legs for him to take a holt of, which was his main dependence in a fight, and then he limped off a piece and laid down and died. It was a good pup, was that Andrew Jackson, and would have made a name for hisself if he'd lived, for the stuff was in him and he had genius—I know it, because he hadn't no opportunities to speak of, and it don't stand to reason that a dog could make such a fight as he could under them circumstances if he hadn't no talent. It always makes me feel sorry when I think of that last fight of his'n, and the way it turned out.

Well, thish-yer Smiley had rat-tarriers, and chicken cocks, and tom-cats and all of them kind of things, till you couldn't rest, and you couldn't fetch nothing for him to bet on but he'd match you. He ketched a frog one day, and took him home, and said he cal'klated to educate him; and so he never done nothing for three months but set in his back yard and learn that frog to jump. And you bet you he *did* learn him, too. He'd give him a little punch behind, and the next minute you'd see that frog whirling in the air like a doughnut—see him turn one summerset, or may be a couple, if got a good start, and come down flat-footed and all right, like a cat. He got him up so in the matter of ketching flies, and kep' him in practice so constant, that he'd nail a fly every time as far as he could see him. Smiley said all a frog wanted was education, and he could do 'most anything—and I believe him. Why, I've seen him set Dan'l Webster down here on this floor—Dan'l Webster was the name of the frog—and sing out, "Flies, Dan'l, flies!" and quicker'n you could wink he'd spring straight up and snake a fly off'n the counter there, and flop down on the floor ag'in as solid as a gob of mud, and fall to scratching the side of his head with his hind foot as indifferent as if he hadn't no idea he'd been doin' any more'n any frog might do. You never see a frog so modest and straightfor'ard and he was, for all he was so gifted. And when it come to fair and square jumping on a dead level, he could get over more ground at one straddle than any animal of his breed you ever see. Jumping on a dead level was his strong suit, you understand; and when it come to that, Smiley would ante up money on him as long as he had a red. Smiley was monstrous proud of his frog, and well he might be, for fellers that had traveled and been everywheres, all he said he laid over any frog that ever *they* see.

Well, Smiley kep'n the beast in a little lattice box, and he used to fetch him down town sometimes and lay for a bet. One day a feller—a stranger in the camp, he was—come acrost him with his box, and says:

"What might it be that you've got in the box?"

And Smiley says, sorter indifferent-like, "It might be a parrot, or it might be a canary, maybe, but it ain't—it's only just a frog."

And the feller took it, and looked at it careful, and turned it round this way and that, and says, "H'm—so 'tis. Well, what's *he* good for?"

"Well," Smiley says, easy and careless, "he's good enough for *one* thing, I should judge—he can outjump any frog in Calaveras county."

The feller took the box again, and took another long, particular look, and give it back to Smiley, and says, very deliberate, "Well," he says, "I don't see no p'ints about that frog that says better'n any other frog."

"Maybe you don't," Smiley says. "Maybe you understand frogs and maybe you don't understand 'em; maybe you've had experience, and maybe you ain't only a amature, as it were. Anyways, I've got *my* opinion and I'll risk forty dollars that he can outjump any frog in Calaveras county."

And the feller studied a minute, and the says, kinder sad like, "Well, I'm only a stranger here, and I ain't got no frog; but if I had a frog, I'd bet you."

And then Smiley says, "That's all right—that's all right—if you'll hold my box a minute, I'll go and get you a frog." And so the feller took the box, and put up his forty dollars along with Smiley's, and set down to wait.

So he set there a good while thinking and thinking to hisself, and then he got the frog out and prized his mouth open and took a teaspoon and filled him full of quail shot—filled him pretty near up to his chin—and set him on the floor. Smiley he went to the swamp and slopped around in the mud for a long time, and finally he ketched a frog, and fetched him in, and give him to this feller, and says:

"Now, if you're ready, set him along side of Dan'l, with his forepaws just even with Dan'l's, and I'll give the word." Then he says, "One—two—three—*git!*" and him and the other feller touched up the frogs from behind, and the new frog hopped off lively, but Dan'l give a heave, and hysted up his shoulders—so—like a Frenchman, but it warn't no use—he couldn't budge; he was

planted as solid as a church, and he couldn't no more stir than if he was anchored out. Smiley was a good deal surprised, and he was disgusted too, but he didn't have no idea what the matter was, of course.

The feller took the money and started away; and when he was going out at the door, he sorter jerked his thumb over his shoulder—so—at Dan'l, and says again, very deliberate, "Well," he says, "*I* don't see no p'ints about that frog that's any better'n any other frog."

Smiley he stood scratching his head and looking down at Dan'l a long time, and at last he says, "I do wonder what in the nation that frog throwed off for—I wonder if there ain't something the matter with him—he 'pears to look mighty baggy, somehow." And he ketched Dan'l by the nap of the neck, and hefted him, and says, "Why blame my cats if he don't weigh five pounds!" and turned him upside down and he belched out a double handful of shot. And then he see how it was, and he was the maddest man—he set the frog down and took out after that feller, but he never ketched him. And—"

[Here Simon Wheeler heard his name called from the front yard,

and got up to see what was wanted.] And turning to me as he moved away, he said: "Just set where you are, stranger, and rest easy—I ain't going to be gone a second."

But, by your leave, I did not think that a continuation of the history of the enterprising vagabond *Jim* Smiley would be likely to afford me much information concerning the Rev. *Leonidas W.* Smiley, and so I started away.

At the door I met the sociable Wheeler returning, and he button-holed me and re-commenced:

"Well, thish-yer Smiley had a yaller one-eyed cow that didn't have no tail, only jest a short stump like a bannanner, and—"

However, lacking both time and inclination, I did not wait to hear about the afflicted cow, but took my leave.

A MARK TWAIN TIME LINE

1835   Samuel L. Clemens is born a few miles west of the Mississippi River in a country palace in Florida, Missouri, November 30. Visiting his birthplace years later, as the famous author Mark Twain, he was surprised to discover that the palace was only a two-room frontier cabin. Andrew Jackson is president. Halley's comet streaks across the sky in slow motion.

1839   The Clemens family moves to nearby Hannibal, Missouri, on the west bank of the great Mississippi River. Twain will use his hometown scenery as backdrop for his immortal novels *Tom Sawyer* and *Huckleberry Finn*.

1847   Twain's father dies. America is at war with Mexico.

1848   Mark claims to have landed a job, at starvation wages, as an apprentice printer, age fourteen, on Joseph Ament's *Hannibal Courier*. Most likely this occurred two years later. He is unaware that his literary career is beginning.

1849   Spends his last day in school, according to myth, and begins to educate himself. Raw material for his novel about Tom Sawyer is accumulating, although he doesn't know it. The California Gold Rush is under way. Edgar Allen Poe dies. Zachary Taylor is president.

1850   Works on his brother's newspaper in Hannibal. Mark is unable to collect his salary, but he has become a skilled typesetter. He will pursue the printer's trade for several years. Nathaniel Hawthorne's classic novel *The Scarlet Letter* is published. Millard Fillmore is now president, the sixth in Twain's young life.

1853–1856   A tramp printer, Twain ranges as far as New York City to scrape together a living. Writes an occasional piece of newspaper humor under such fanciful names as W. Epaminondas Blab and Thomas Jefferson Snodgrass. The world little notices.

1857   A boyhood dream comes true. Twain becomes minor royalty as a cub pilot on the Mississippi River.

1858   Mark persuades his beloved younger brother, Henry, to take a lowly job on the steamboat *Pennsylvania*. In June, the ship explodes and Henry is killed. Twain never forgives himself for luring Henry to his death.

1859   Twain receives his license as a steamboat pilot. Discovers Tom Paine, whose writing energized the American Revolution.

Twain begins to doubt the parlor bigotries of his childhood.

1861   The Civil War breaks out. Twain decamps for the far west with his brother Orion. Eleven years later, he transforms the twenty-one-day stagecoach trip into his best-selling book, *Roughing It*.

1862   In Virginia City he begins writing for the *Daily Territorial Enterprise*. He claims to have discovered a petrified man. Civil War rages on.

1863   Lincoln delivers the Gettysburg Address.

1864   Sam fights duel, some believe; flees to San Francisco. Reporter for the *Morning Call.*

1865   Prospects for gold around Jackass Hill and Angel's Camp, California. After false start, Clemens firmly adopts the pen name Mark Twain on the story that would make him famous, "The Celebrated Jumping Frog of Calaveras County" (pronounced cal-a-VER-us). Civil War ends.

1866   Sails for the Sandwich Islands. Returning to San Francisco, Twain gives his first public lecture, warning: "The Trouble to begin at 8 o'clock."

1867   He joins pilgrims aboard the *Quaker City* on a trip to the Mediterranean and the Holy Land.

1868 Writes his first book, *The Innocents Abroad,* in two months. Bids farewell to San Francisco and the West; goes east. Former slaves granted citizenship. Ulysses S. Grant is elected president.

1870 Marries Olivia Langdon. Confederate general Robert E. Lee dies. So does Charles Dickens.

1872 *Roughing It* published. Twain's infant son, Langdon, dies.

1874 Begins writing *Tom Sawyer;* finishes the following year. Daughter Clara is born.

1876 Begins writing *Adventures of Huckleberry Finn;* Seven years pass before he finishes the manuscript. *The Adventures of Tom Sawyer* is published.

1878 Moves his family to Europe for the next two years.

1881 Publishes *The Prince and the Pauper.*

1883 Finishes writing *Adventures of Huckleberry Finn. Life on the Mississippi* is published. So is Robert Louis Stevenson's *Treasure Island.* The volcano Krakatoa erupts in Indonesia, shooting dust around the world.

1885 Twain is fifty years old. Heavy lecturing schedule. Publishes *Adventures of Huckleberry Finn.* Grover Cleveland is president.

1889   Publishes *A Connecticut Yankee in King Arthur's Court*. Nellie Bly creates a sensation by traveling around the world in less than eighty days.

1890   Twain's mother dies.

1891   Moves with his family to Europe. Is troubled with rheumatism; learns to write with his left hand.

1894   Publishes *Pudd'nhead Wilson*. Notorious trial of Alfred Dreyfus in France.

1895   Returns with family to the United States. Bankrupted by his investment in a typesetting machine, he launches a round-the-world lecture tour to pay off his debts.

1896   His daughter Susy dies.

1897   Orion Clemens dies.

1904   His wife, Livy, dies.

1909   Twain is discovered to have heart disease. His daughter Jean dies.

1910   Samuel L. Clemens dies at sunset, April 21. Halley's comet returns for the occasion.

Halley's comet, photographed in 1910, the year Mark Twain joined the immortals.

REFERENCES

ABBREVIATIONS:

Auto	*The Autobiography of Mark Twain*
Fatout	*Mark Twain Speaking,* Paul Fatout
Illustrated	*Mark Twain, an Illustrated Biography,* Geoffrey Ward et al.
Innocents	*The Innocents Abroad*
Kaplan	*Mr. Clemens and Mark Twain,* Justin Kaplan
Letters	*Mark Twain's Letters from Hawaii,* A. Grove Day
Miss	*Life on the Mississippi*
Paine	*Mark Twain,* Albert Bigelow Paine
Portable	*The Portable Mark Twain,* Bernard de Voto (ed.)
Powers	*Mark Twain, A Life,* Ron Powers
Puddn'head	*Puddn'head Wilson*
Roughing	*Roughing It*
Sanborn	*Mark Twain: The Bachelor Years,* Margaret Sanborn
Wit	*The Wit and Wisdom of Mark Twain*

Where there are multiple editions of a work, such as *Roughing It*, I have avoided the chaos of page numbers by assigning quotes to their chapters.

A Horror of Introductions

Page

xi "I was obliged . . ." Fatout, p. 4

xi "I don't know anything . . . I don't know why." Sanborn, p. 300

xiii "The Trouble to begin at 8 o'clock." 1866 advertisement

Chapter 1: The Man Who Made Frogs Famous

3 "most killed themselves laughing." Sanborn, p. 260

"It was only the frog . . . It wasn't I." Auto, p. 199

4 "Man is the only animal . . ." *Pudd'nhead*

4 "Cauliflower is . . ." Ibid.

4 "Everybody complains . . ." *The Gilded Age*

4 "almost invisible." Auto, p. I

Chapter 2: Eggs, Three Cents a Dozen

10 "When I first . . ." Powers, p. 8

10 "If the jaw remained . . ." Auto, p. 14

10 "I suppose that . . . afraid you would." Ibid., p. 15

15 "In my schoolboy . . . settle his mind" Ibid., p. 8

15 "Man—a creature . . ." Portable

Chapter 3: The Gingerbread Kid

18 "She was looking . . . in that town." Auto, p. 42

"It roused her scorn . . . to reform." Ibid., p. 16

19 "But a boy's life . . ." Auto, p. 53

19 "Because I had a delicacy . . ." Sanborn, p. 53

19 "I fancied . . . so I took it." *Innocents*, chapter 18

23 "It is all right . . . break my heart." Paine, p. 75

24 "I discount him . . ." Sanborn, p. 33

CHAPTER 4: UPSIDE DOWN AND BACKWARD

25 "I was only . . ." Auto, p. 115

32 "Terrible Accident . . . (To be Continued.)" Sanborn, pp. 77–78

32 "failing to drink himself to death." Sanborn, p. 74

33 "I want you to repeat . . ." Paine, p. 93

34 "I made up my mind . . ." Auto, p. 128

34 "that there weren't any . . ." Ibid., p. 128

CHAPTER 5: THE RIVERBOAT RAJAH

35 "How would you like . . . when I earn it." Paine, pp. 117–118

37 "What's the name . . . a cow down a lane." Miss, chapter 6

40 "couldn't get the bottom . . . immortal *soul* out of her." Ibid., chapter 13

41 "Oh, Ben . . ." Ibid., chapter 13

CHAPTER 6: THE CRUEL RIVER

43 "till the last . . ." Miss, chapter 15

44 "It was a large experience." Ibid., chapter 24

46 "But Sid was . . ." Auto, p. 43

CHAPTER 7: SAM AND THE FORTUNE-TELLER

48 "in making those idiots . . ." *Innocents*, chapter 6

50 "I don't believe . . ." Sanborn, p. 59

51 "I loved the . . ." Paine, p. 162

52 "You are self-made . . . Don't interrupt." Ibid., p. 158

52 "just as good . . ." Ibid., p. 157

52 "Prophecy . . ." Wit, p. 186

CHAPTER 8: TWO WEEKS AS A WARRIOR

55 "I'm not . . ." Paine, p. 161

57 "incapacitated by fatigue." Auto, p. 134

57 "buffaloes and Indians . . ." *Roughing*, chapter 1

59 "a good deal of a nuisance." Auto, p. 134

CHAPTER 9: THE BUFFALO THAT CLIMBED A TREE

62 "I thought it was grand . . ." *Roughing*, chapter 2

63 "Long after he was . . ." Ibid., chapter 3

63 "but as a vegetable . . ." Ibid., chapter 3

64 "as if issued from a cannon." Ibid., chapter 4

64 "sped away toward . . ." Ibid., chapter 7

65 "blaspheming my luck . . . death of a dog if it isn't." Ibid., chapter 7

67 "that after the Indians were gone . . ." *Roughing*, chapter 97

67 "Our breakfast. . ." Ibid., chapter 4

68 "Never youth stared . . . filling my cup." Ibid., chapter 4

CHAPTER 10: THIEVES, MURDERERS, AND DESPERADOES

70 "Nothing helps scenery . . ." *Roughing*, chapter 17

70 "The sun beat down . . . forsaken than before." Ibid., chapter 18

70 "concentrated hideousness" Ibid., chapter 18

70 "because we never . . ." Ibid, chapter 18

71 "It never rains . . . provisions with them." Paine, chapter 32

71 "Thieves, murderers, desperadoes . . . jackass rabbits." Ibid., chapter 32

72 "All quiet . . . " Ibid., chapter 32

72 "He has a general . . . the mail sacks." *Roughing*, chapter 5

75 "like sheet music." Ibid., chapter 21

75 "frenzied as the craziest." Paine, chapter 33

CHAPTER 11: GOLD, TEN CENTS AN ACRE

76 "Hurry, was the word!" *Roughing*, chapter 27

76 "I confess . . . the mountain summits." Ibid., chapter 28

77 "granite rubbish . . ." Ibid., chapter 28

77 "One week . . ." Ibid., chapter 29

79 "The whole situation . . ." Ibid., chapter 33

CHAPTER 12: SAM AND THE PETRIFIED MAN

80 "impossible to print . . ." Paine, p. 203

82 "I had been . . . limit on it." *Roughing*, chapter 42

83 "nobody knew anything." Ibid, chapter 42

84 "stirring news" Ibid., chapter 42

84 "pensive" Powers p. 112

87 "Our Heavenly Father . . ." Auto

87 "If you pick up . . ." *Pudd'nhead*, chapter 18

87 "April 1 . . ." Ibid.

CHAPTER 13: THE DUEL AT DAWN

89 "a liar . . ." Sanborn, p. 236

90 "but of the impromptu kind." Paine, chapter 45

90 "One. . . three. . . " Ibid.

90 "Just then . . . twice that far." Ibid.

CHAPTER 14: SAM IN THE BIG CITY

94 "with a step . . ." *Roughing*, chapter 58

95 "the washerwoman's paper." Lauber, p. 136

97 "raking" Auto, p. 156

97 "with considerable warmth . . ." Auto, p. 157

98 "All I care to know . . ." Mark Twain Notebook #42

98 "Concerning the difference . . ." Mark Twain Notebook, 1896

CHAPTER 15: THE SLOUCHING MAN

100 "Mark was the laziest . . . I ever knew." Lauber, p. 139

100 "I became . . . smooth with handling." *Roughing*, chapter 59

101 "Get your facts . . ." Wit, p. 73

104 "Heaven on the half-shell." Powers, p. 143

104 "occupants of adjoining rooms . . ." Wit, p. 105

104 "used to be a good . . ." *Innocents*, vol. 2, chapter 2

105 "Suppose you were . . ." Paine, vol. 2, p. 724

CHAPTER 16: THE TALKING BLUEJAY

110–112 The BlueJay Yarn. *A Tramp Abroad*, chapter 3

CHAPTER 17: THE WATER BOY FROM JACKASS HILL

113 "snoring like a steamboat." *Roughing*, chapter 61

113 "panned up and down . . ." Ibid., chapter 61

115 "Jim . . . I won't carry . . . in that pan." Paine, p. 270

Chapter 18: Good-bye, Sam; Hello, Mark
121 "The sketch scored . . ." Powers, p. 154

Chapter 19: The Sandwich Chronicles
126 "I took a tranquil delight . . ." Letters, #1
126 "That's all right—" Ibid.
127 "I could have shaved . . ." *Roughing*, chapter 63
127 "I saw cats . . ." Letters, #4
128 "two million mosquitoes . . ." Ibid., #1
128 "convulsive" *Roughing*, chapter 64
128 "I have a delicacy about sitting down." Ibid., chapter 64
129 "on stilts" Ibid., chapter 64
129 "I breathed in . . ." *Roughing*, chapter 63
129 "Nothing so needs . . ." *Pudd'nhead*, chapter 15
130 "The board struck. . . ." *Roughing*, chapter 73
130 "went and sat down . . ." Letters, #21
130 "luxurious vagrancy" *Roughing*, chapter 78
132 "toiling up the hill . . . you got it." Letters, #21

Chapter 20: The Trouble Begins at 8
134 "I returned to California . . ." Auto, p. 187
134 "The coldest winter . . ." Attributed to Mark Twain
135 "strike while the iron . . ." Auto, p. 187
136 "And charge . . ." *Roughing*, chapter 78
137 "The Trouble to begin . . ." Ibid., Appendix D
137 "A Splendid Orchestra . . . whatever they please." Paine, p. 292
139 "The tumult . . ." *Roughing*, chapter 78
140 "he wasn't going to . . ." Fatout, p. 4

140 "The natives . . . illustrate the matter." Ibid., pp. 8–10

CHAPTER 21: THE GREAT HOLDUP

144 "Keep your seat . . ." Auto, pp. 189-191

145 "a horrible six-shooter . . ." *Roughing*, chapter 79

145 "My son, your arguments . . . put up my hands." Ibid.

148 "unruffled as a mountain lake" Paine, p. 300

148 "mad clear through" Ibid., p. 300

CHAPTER 22: TWAIN ATTEMPTS TO BEHAVE

150 "This son of . . ." Wit, p. vii

151 "The Wisdom will begin . . ." Paine, vol 3, p. 1604

154 "to fill a nail keg." *Innocents*, p. 17

154 "Do you wonder . . ." Paine, p. 336

156 "a funeral excursion. . ." Illustrated, p. 69

CHAPTER 23: GOLDEN GATE, SO LONG

160 "some of the wind and water" Auto, p. 195

160 "I did 200,000 words . . ." Ibid., p. 195

161 "The report of my death . . ." Wit, p. 55

161 "Mark Twain, God Knows Where." Goldfarb family letter, 1915 (copy supplied to author by a descendent, Robert Goldfarb)

161 "He did." Ibid.

CHAPTER 24: AFTERSTORY

165 "Everyone complains . . ." *The Gilded Age*

166 "Notice . . . will be shot." *Adventures of Huckleberry Finn*

166 "The Widow Douglas . . ." Ibid.

167 "If I'd a knowed . . ." Ibid.

170 "tolerably well" Kaplan, p. 199

172 "The difference . . ." Letters, 1888

172 "When in doubt . . ." Pudd'nhead Wilson's new calendar, Portable

174 "A successful book . . ." Letter to W. D. Howells, 1887

174 "the American Shakespeare . . ." *Booklist*

175 "I have been . . ." Letter to W. D. Howells, 1887

THE TRUTH, MORE OR LESS

177 "A lie well told . . ." Speech, 1882

179 "When I was a boy . . . in seven years." Wit, p. 75

180 "A lie can travel . . ." Attributed to Mark Twain

ILLUSTRATION AND PHOTOGRAPH SOURCES

THE AUTHOR WISHES TO EXPRESS DELIGHT AND gratitude for the many institutions with Mark Twain collections who graciously made selections available for this biography.

Library of Congress

pp. i, 141. "'Mark Twain,' America's best humorist." Illustration by Joseph Ferdinand Keppler, *Puck* (December 16, 1885, v.18), p. 256.

p. 8. "Mark Twain's birthplace, Fla., Mo." George Grantham Bain Collection, Bain News Service, publisher.

p. 20. "Mark Twain House, Hannibal, MO." Photo from the Historic American Buildings Survey, 1933–, exact date unknown.

p. 39. "The Champions of the Mississippi," detail. Illustration by Fanny Palmer, published by Currier & Ives, New York (1866).

p. 45. "Saint Louis, MO. in 1855." Engraving on stone by Leopold Gast & Brother, 1855.

p. 47. "Burning of the steamer *Stonewall*, on the Mississippi River." Illustration from *Frank Leslie's Illustrated Newspaper* (November 13, 1869), p. 149.

p. 53. "The Symbolical head, illustrating all the phrenological developments of the human head." Fowler & Strachan, 1842.

p. 81. "Mark Twain 'Enterprise' Building, Virginia City, NV." Photo by Robert W. Kerrigan from the Historic American Buildings Survey, 1933–, exact date unknown.

p. 86. "Cemetery, Virginia City, NV." Photo by N. L. McAfee from the Historic American Buildings Survey, May 1940.

p. 96. "Folsom & Second Streets, Historic View, San Francisco, CA." Photo from the Historic American Buildings Survey, 1856.

p. 108. "Mark Twain Cabin, Jackass Hill, Tuolumne County, CA." Photocopy of photograph (late 19th century, before restoration) from the Historic American Buildings Survey, 1933–, exact date unknown.

p. 108. "Mark Twain Cabin, Jackass Hill, Tuolumne County, CA." Photocopy of photograph (restored cabin, date unknown) from the Historic American Buildings Survey, 1933–, exact date unknown.

p. 120. "Fardon, East Side of Montgomery Street." Historic American Buildings Survey, Wells Fargo Bank Historical Museum Photo, 1856.

p. 147. "Frederick House, D Street, Virginia City, NV." Photo from the Historic American Buildings Survey, 1933–, exact date unknown.

p. 158. "Samuel Langhorne Clemens, three-quarter length portrait." Photo taken between 1900–1910, first published in 1941.

p. 173. "Mark Twain, head-and-shoulders portrait." Photo by T. E. Marr (1903), from Curtis Publishing Co.

Mark Twain's Works

pp. 20 (top), 21, 31 (both), 122 (bottom), 169. All illustrations by E. W. Kemble from the first edition of *Adventures of Huckleberry Finn*, Charles L. Webster & Co., 1885.

p. 12. Illustration by True Williams from the first American edition of *The Adventures of Tom Sawyer*, American Publishing Company, Hartford, CT, 1876.

pp. 58, 116, 182, 190, 192. All illustrations from *The Celebrated Jumping Frog of Calaveras County*, published in *Mark Twain's Sketches, New and Old*. American Publishing Company, Hartford, CT, 1875.

p. 81 (top), 86 (top), 138. Images courtesy of the Nevada Historical Society in Reno, Nevada.

pp. 45, 103. Photos courtesy of Brown Brothers.

p. 125. Photo courtesy of the Yale Collection of American Literature, Beinecke Rare Book and Manuscript Library, Yale University.

p. 159 (bottom). Photo from author's personal collection.

p. 197. US Postal Service.

p. 199. Photo courtesy of the Bishop Museum, Honolulu, Hawaii.

BIBLIOGRAPHY

I HAVE NO GRUDGE AGAINST THE ALPHABET; I LIVE by it. But in this listing of books about Mark Twain, I felt that it would be misleading to call in the ABC's to impose a marching order. Instead, I have chosen to arrange my sources according to the magnitude of their charm for me as a reader and their usefulness to me as a biographer.

Twain, Mark, edited by Charles Neider. *The Autobiography of Mark Twain.* New York: Harper and Brothers, 1959.
Logically enough, these are the pages I turned to when first seized with the notion of attempting a new life of the great man. I discovered that he spared no effort in passing along bewitching inaccuracies about himself. In short, he could be enjoyed, but not trusted. I consulted less gifted but more reliable Twain scholars.

Paine, Albert Bigelow. *Mark Twain: A Biography.* New York: Chelsea House, 1980.
Paine, a close friend, spent the last few years living under the same roof

with Twain, taking notes for a detailed biography. It is devotional, but Paine does tweak the author here and there. He consults Twain's old friends to correct or expand on the writer's imaginative memory.

Powers, Ron. *Mark Twain: A Life.* New York: Free Press/Simon and Schuster, 2005.
Elegant. Brings facts up to date with superlative scholarship, rendered with style.

Rasmussen, R. Kent. *Mark Twain A to Z.* New York: Oxford University Press, 1995.
An essential research book, always at my elbow. Any detail in Twain's life, no matter how remote, is here tracked down. The patient author should receive a chest full of medals for curiosity, care, and persistence.

Ward, Geoffrey C., Ken Burns, and Dayton Duncan. *Mark Twain: An Illustrated Biography.* New York: Knopf, 2001.
A feast of photographs and contemporary illustrations, many of which have been buried away in collections for a century or more. A skilled text.

Sanborn, Margaret. *Mark Twain: The Bachelor Years.* New York: Doubleday, 1990.
A probing, engaging account of the years of the author's life prior to his marriage.

Lennon, Nigey. *Mark Twain in California* (The Literary West series). San Francisco: Chronicle Books, 1982.
A delight. A reader-friendly account by a writer whose only qualification is the best of all: "delirium Clemens."

Benson, Ivan. *Mark Twain's Western Years.* Stanford, CA: Stanford University Press, 1938.

A straightforward account.

Day, A. Grove, editor. *Mark Twain's Letters from Hawaii.* Honolulu: The University Press of Hawaii, 1966.

Letters, in newspaper parlance, meant articles. This, together with Twain's rendering in *Roughing It,* gave me a fix on the Sandwich Islands episodes. In his autobiography, Twain edited out the tropics.

Fatout, Paul, editor. *Mark Twain Speaking.* Iowa City: University of Iowa Press, 1976.

A copy was elusive, but worth the search. Here was Mark onstage, in person, breathing fire and setting off laughs.

DeVoto, Bernard, editor. *The Portable Mark Twain.* New York: Viking, 1946.

Like Frankenstein's monster, a book made up from parts of other Twain books. A volume to skip around in or skip entirely in favor of the original texts.

———. *Mark Twain in Eruption.* New York: Harper and Brothers, 1940.

A collection of memories and opinions that Twain left out of his autobiography.

Mason, Miriam E. *Mark Twain, Young Writer* (Childhood of Famous Americans). New York: Aladdin, 1991.

Scenes that never happened, imaginary dialogue. Well-intentioned misfire, first published in 1942. Keep out of the hands of children.

Ayres, Alex, editor. *The Wit and Wisdom of Mark Twain.* New York: HarperPerennial, 1987.

A book of one-liners.

Kaplan, Justin. *Mr. Clemens and Mark Twain: A Biography.* New York: Simon & Schuster, 2003.

A good book, but unfortunately picks up Twain's life from the year Clemens left San Francisco forever, which is where my tale largely ends.

THE NOVELS AND OTHER WORKS

Each of Mark Twain's books can be found in a great variety of printings. I have favored the editions in the Mark Twain Library, University of California Press, published in the 1980s and 1990s. They contain illustrations from the original editions. No matter the edition, Twain remains fresh and whimsical. Here are a few of his works referred to in my text, with dates of first publication:

The Innocents Abroad (American Publishing Company, 1869)

Roughing It (American Publishing Company, 1872)

The Gilded Age: A Tale of Today, with Charles Dudley Warner (American Publishing Company, 1873)

The Adventures of Tom Sawyer (American Publishing Company, 1876)

A Tramp Abroad (American Publishing Company, 1880)

The Prince and the Pauper (James R. Osgood & Company, 1882)

Life on the Mississippi (James R. Osgood & Company, 1883)

Adventures of Huckleberry Finn (Charles L. Webster & Co., 1885)

A Connecticut Yankee in King Arthur's Court (Charles L. Webster & Co., 1889)

The Tragedy of Pudd'nhead Wilson (American Publishing Company, 1894)

INDEX

• • •

· · ·